THE LEADERSHIP DIET

THE 21 HEALTH LAWS OF LEADERSHIP

Follow Them and Regain Your Health, Lower Your Stress and Boost Your Energy!

JERRY L. ANDERSON

What people say about

THE LEADERSHIP DIET

The Leadership Diet is riveting reading! It's full of practical advice on how to strengthen your leadership abilities by focusing on healthy eating. The 21 irrefutable principles of health turn into 21 drivers for enhanced leadership! Everyone—from clerks to CEO's—can become masters of their own destiny by following Jerry's down-to-earth advice that works!

Bev Thorne, Chief Marketing Officer

I love the fact that you did your research and did not make false statements. I also love that it is a conversational piece; I could hear your voice in my head as I read through the text. This will, no doubt, serve to help many individuals get on the right road to healthier lives.

Joyce M. Richey, Ph.D.
AP of Clinical Physiology & Neuroscience

Jerry, I can say those 21 health principles have brought about a change and discipline in my life and have revealed to me that I can live longer and not die before God's time. A must read for everyone.

Dr. Michael C. Brown, Senior Pastor
St. John's Baptist Church

Awesome read! Very motivational. Thank you, Jerry, for the upfront, in-your-face statistics and challenges. Thank you, Jerry, for having a heart for the people and caring enough to share these 21 Health Laws with us. I am able to take something very significant from each health law and apply to my daily life. Now it's time for me to implement my "call for action." What a blessing!

Valerie Andrews, RN-Nurse Educator

Your leadership will never surpass your personal health. You have one shot with your life so take your best shot! This book will teach you how. The Leadership Diet extends a compelling vision for your life. It calls you up! Yet, it tells you how to get there. Live it! Share with others like it really matters.

Dr. Ronnie Floyd, Senior Pastor
Cross Church

The Leadership Diet is easy to understand with many great reasons for why we should treat our bodies as our personal temple. The book will clearly help the user gain positive results with laid out how and why. Jerry you really talk the talk and walk the walk with this book all your examples are so easy to understand.

Anne Marie Knudsen, RN, Clinical Nurse Specialist

Warning! Reading this book will compel you to action. You will be enlightened and inspired along the journey toward living a healthy and whole life by caring for your mind, body and spirit. I love how the principles of health are presented in such a clear and practical way! This book, like the author, is a great motivator!

Dr. RaShaye Freeman, Doctor of Nursing Practice

This is an eye-opening book. The 21 steps are informative and succinct with fun, interesting anecdotes. All the top advice on healthy living in one place!

Maxine Thomas, Master of Science
Instructional Performance Technology

"As a leader, I've learned that managing my energy may be even more important than managing my time. Jerry Anderson has provided a enjoyable, accessible book that rings with the truth of scripture. As leaders in every arena understand and apply these laws, whole communities will continue to grow, transform, and heal."
Dr. Seth Pickens, Senior Pastor
Zion Hill Baptist Church

The Leadership Diet is as informative and energetic as Brother Jerry Anderson! He has a passion for teaching leaders to be healthy, and I'm glad he finally wrote a book so he can reach the people who can't reach him. The information in his book is very much needed for all leaders. He doesn't just tell us to get healthy. He gives us the how-to and tells us what will happen if we don't. He encourages us in writing the way he does in a workout by telling us how it has worked for others. Thank you, Brother Jerry! This book is a treasure!

Rev. Jacquetta Y. Parhams, Ph.D.
Founder, The Whole-Self Ministries

I met Jerry Anderson when he spoke to our Leadership Summit in Arkansas. I have been an avid runner and cyclist for 30 years. After listening to Jerry I took his advice and I improved my physical, emotional and mental strength, daily work performance and overall health. I highly recommend *The Leadership Diet*–it's practical, helpful and can save your life!

Andy Wilson, Chief Executive Office
Former Executive Leader of Wal-Mart Stores

This book is a must have! It is life changing, because it is the portrait of a life lived. The author is not just another research guru interested in making a profit. He has lived by these laws and has helped leaders like myself, to do the same.

Dr. Edward A. Ellis, Ph.D.

The Leadership Diet

Library of Congress Control Number: 2017916944

Jerry L. Anderson, Las Vegas, NV

ISBN: 13: 978-0692973486

1. Leadership. 2. Industrial Management.

Cover Design by: Carolyn Sheltraw

DISCLAIMER: This book is not intended to take the place of medical advice and treatment from your personal physician. Readers are to consult their own doctor or other qualified professional regarding the treatment of their medical problems. Neither the publisher nor the author takes any responsibility for any possible consequences from any exercise or nutrition advice to any person reading or following the information in this book.

Jerry L. Anderson

To the millions of people to whom I've taught health to over the years through radio, television conferences, meetings, and personal trainings···

And to you—

The person wanting to become a healthier Business Leader, Church Leader, Manager, Supervisor, Team Leader, Sales Professional, Teacher, CEO, CMO, COO, Administrator, Attorney, Police Officer, Journalist, Doctor, Sales Manager, Singer, Social Worker, Student, Author, Comedian, Meeting Planner, Speaker, Mom or Dad

because

Your Health is the Foundation of Leadership.

Contents

MEASURE YOUR WAISTLINE: You will learn why men and women with large waistlines are more likely to die early. You will learn how to achieve a healthy waistline for life. You will learn why an overweight billionaire died at the age of 41.

HAVE A HEALTHY BREAKFAST: You will learn how eating an unhealthy breakfast can make you overweight and unnourished. You will learn how having a healthy breakfast will fuel you with all the energy you need to start your day with high energy for maximum productivity. You will learn how the guy who had a healthy breakfast every morning lost twenty pounds and four inches off his waistline in six weeks.

SKIP THE SOFT DRINKS: You will learn how having one soda a day may increase your waistline by five inches in one year. You will learn the importance of skipping the soft drinks. You will learn how skipping the soft drinks can help you lose ten inches off your waistline in one year.

PACK SOME RESISTANCE: You will learn how not exercising when you travel reduces your mental capacity. You will learn how packing some resistance will help you keep your exercise habit in place when you are traveling. You will learn how Arnold Schwarzenegger packs resistance when he travels.

SLOW DOWN YOUR EATING SPEED: You will learn how eating fast may cause you to become a diabetic. You will learn how slowing down your eating speed will prevent you from overeating. You will learn why the fastest eater at the table is usually the heaviest one at the table.

THE NINTH HEALTH LAW OF LEADERSHIP   74

WALK AT WORK: You will learn why not walking at work may cause you to have blood pooling and varicose veins. You will learn how walking at work will energize you throughout the day. You will learn how a sales manager lost forty pounds and eight inches off his waistline in six months by walking at work.

THE TENTH HEALTH LAW OF LEADERSHIP   80

SUPERSIZE YOUR SALAD AT LUNCH: You will learn how not supersizing your salad can supersize your waistline. You will learn how supersizing your salad at lunch will ensure you to stay energized, alert, and productive in the afternoon. You will learn how a guy supersized his salad at lunch for a year and a half and lost 95 pounds and 19 inches off his waistline.

THE ELEVENTH HEALTH LAW OF LEADERSHIP   84

BUILD YOUR MUSCLES: You will learn why you tend to gain weight as we get older. You will learn how weight lifting can help you build muscle and improve your appearance. You will learn how one of my clients gained fifteen pounds of muscle and lost three inches off her waistline in six months.

STAY MENTALLY FIT: You will learn how negative thinking can reduce your life span. You will learn how staying mentally fit will improve your physical well-being and psychological health. You will learn how a guy changed his mindset and changed his body in 15 minutes.

EAT MORE FRUIT AND VEGETABLES: You will learn how 7.8 million premature deaths each year worldwide can be avoided. You will learn why eating fruits and vegetables will lower your chances of heart attack, stroke, cancer, and early death. You will learn how a celebrity lost 100 pounds in one year eating fruits and vegetables, and then gained it all back.

TRACK YOUR FIBER: You will learn why a low fiber intake will shorten your life and increase your possibility of diseases. You will learn that increasing your fiber intake may control your blood sugar levels and minimize inflammation throughout your body. You will learn how one of my clients started tracking his fiber and lost forty pounds and eight inches off his waistline in six months.

THE EIGHTEENTH HEALTH LAW OF LEADERSHIP   122

AVOID FAD DIETS: You will learn why fad diets are potentially dangerous. You will learn the six ways to expose a fad diet. You will learn how a guy who was overweight with health issues tried a fad diet and died.

THE NINETEENTH HEALTH LAW OF LEADERSHIP   128

SET REALISTIC WEIGHT LOSS GOALS: You will learn the top three reasons people fail at achieving their weight loss goals. You will learn how to lose weight safely and keep it off. You will learn how a guy tried to lose 60 pounds in 30 days by eating 800 calories a day.

THE TWENTIETH HEALTH LAW OF LEADERSHIP   135

RELAX AND LAUGH: You will learn how mental stress can cause you to have a heart attack or a stroke. You will learn how relaxing and laughing opens up your blood vessels so they can deliver more blood, oxygen, and nutrients to your cells. You will learn how a woman and her husband were having a heated argument and she got so upset she had a heart attack and died.

Jerry L. Anderson

THE TWENTY-FIRST HEALTH LAW OF LEADERSHIP 142

VISUALIZE YOURSELF SUCCEEDING: You will learn how the wrong mental practice can set you up for failure. You will learn how your nervous system cannot tell the difference between an "actual" experience and an "imagined" experience. You will learn how one of my clients who was scared to enter a competition visualized herself succeeding and won.

Acknowledgments

I'd like to thank the many people who helped me while I was working on this book.

I must thank my Lord and Savior Jesus Christ for the wisdom and creativity to write this book.

I want to thank the writers from healthday.com who published all the great studies cited throughout this book.

I want to say thanks to all the clients I have worked with over the last 30 years and all the people I have talked to at conferences and meetings who have provided the stories in my book.

I want to thank my outstanding editors, Marianne Thompson and Dr. Jacquetta Y. Parhams, for making the book clear and simple.

Finally, I want to give a special thanks to my daughters, Ashley Joy Anderson and Haley Morgan Anderson, for being my greatest inspirations.

Introduction

This book grew from thirty years of coaching clients and speaking at different leadership meetings and conferences. I remember being at the airport on my way to a speaking engagement. I was talking to a hiring director for a Fortune 500 company, and I asked her, "If you had a choice between two potential leaders to hire, one who was a ten in leadership skills and a five on health, and the other one was an eight on leadership skills and an eight on health, which one would you hire?" She said she would hire the one with the eight on leadership skills and eight on health. "The one with the ten on leadership skills and five on health probably would not last. It would be a bad investment."

Listen to this! I was talking to a meeting planner in preparation to speak at his leadership conference, and I asked him, "What is your reason for inviting me to speak to your leadership team?" He said, "Jerry, we realized that just thinking about leadership skills for our leaders was extremely short-sighted. Without your health, you have nothing." Then he went on to say, "You can be the best leader in the whole world, but without your health, everything declines and even stops."

I remember talking to a COO and he told me, "When I was overweight, I always felt like I was letting my team down, my wife down and my daughter down." Then his eyes began watering. Not being

18

healthy really had an emotional impact on his business life and family life. He felt it projected the image of lack of discipline and focus.

On the flip side, I was speaking at a leadership conference and the attendees told me, "Ever since our new CEO has come on board, everyone at the company is taking better care of their health." Their new CEO was very active and fit. He worked out every morning and they knew it, and guess what? His team started working out, improving on their health as well.

At a Pastors' Leadership Conference, several people mentioned to me that pastors were having heart attacks, strokes, and passing out on the pulpit in the middle of their sermon. It shocked me! I recently read about a pastor who had a heart attack in the middle of his sermon and died. The article stated that his congregation thought he looked healthy, but when I saw the accompanying photo of him, he looked like he was 200 pounds overweight!

I enjoy working with pastors on improving their health. One pastor I trained with for three months lost twenty-two pounds of fat and gained twenty pounds of muscle, reduced his waistline by six inches, and increased his energy drastically. And getting healthy inspires others. His assistant pastor then got on board and he lost excess weight improving his health, which then led his deacons to follow who all lost weight, which trickled down to its members who started taking better care of their health.

I know you are constantly improving your leadership skills. My goal is to help you put your leadership skills into a healthy body. When you combine the 21 health laws of leadership with your leadership skills, you are going to become a healthy, fit, and energized leader along with setting a great example for your team, your congregation, and your family. One of my favorite sayings is "Healthy Leaders Get to the Top and Don't Drop!"

I was talking to this woman after one of my speaking engagements and she told me, "Jerry, I heard you speak three times and finally I decided to follow your health laws." In one year, she lost 105 pounds and 21 inches off her waistline. Her friend followed it with her and she lost 62 pounds and 12 inches off her waistline. These health laws of leadership work!

The 21 Health Laws of Leadership are easy to follow. Each chapter has a Health Law, Health Fact, Stories, a Call to Action and ends with a Motivational Health Quote.

While these Health Laws appear to be simple, they will have a great impact on your life.

Do not let the simplicity fool you.

Now, let's get started adding health to your leadership skills!

The First Health Law of Leadership

Measure Your Waistline!

I want you to measure your waistline and write it down in your calendar and do this once a month. This is how we are going to track your progress as you improve your health and wellness.

The Journal of Clinical Epidemiology showed that health risks begin to increase when a woman's waist reaches 31.5 inches and her risk jumps substantially once her waist expands to 35 inches or more.

For men, health risks start to climb at 37 inches, but it becomes a bigger worry once their waists reach or exceed 40 inches. However, these numbers are based on averages and are not always useful for very tall or short people.

Now, take a tape measure and go around your belly button and record your waistline measurement in your calendar.

Ladies, your goal should be to reduce your waistline to less than 30 inches, and guys, your goal should be to reduce your waistline to less than 35 inches. These guidelines were established by the American Cancer Society who led a study published in the Archives of Internal Medicine on healthy waistline measurements.

How many inches do you need to lose to Reduce Your Waistline according to the American Cancer Society guidelines? _____

For every inch you are over your healthy waistline goal is equal to a five pound weight loss on the scale.

How many pounds do you need to lose to get to your healthy waistline goal? _____

The National Center of Health Statistics measured waistline circumference for women and men over the age of 20. The average woman's waistline circumference was 37.5 inches and the average man's waistline circumference was 39.7 inches.

As you can see, the average woman's waistline is 7.5 inches over the American Cancer Society healthy waistline guidelines. The average man's waistline is 4.7 inches over the guidelines.

Research has shown that those who carry more fat around their abdomen also have higher amounts of fat around vital organs like the kidneys, liver, and pancreas. This so-called visceral fat is more "metabolically active" than fat that lies just below the skin and is thought to promote chronic inflammation, which has been linked to high blood pressure, high cholesterol, type 2 diabetes, heart disease, stroke, gallbladder disease, arthritis, breathing problems, sleep apnea, and certain cancers.

Visceral fat is different from subcutaneous fat. Subcutaneous fat is located directly under the skin. Visceral fat, however, is located in the abdomen underneath the muscle and around vital organs (see photo below).

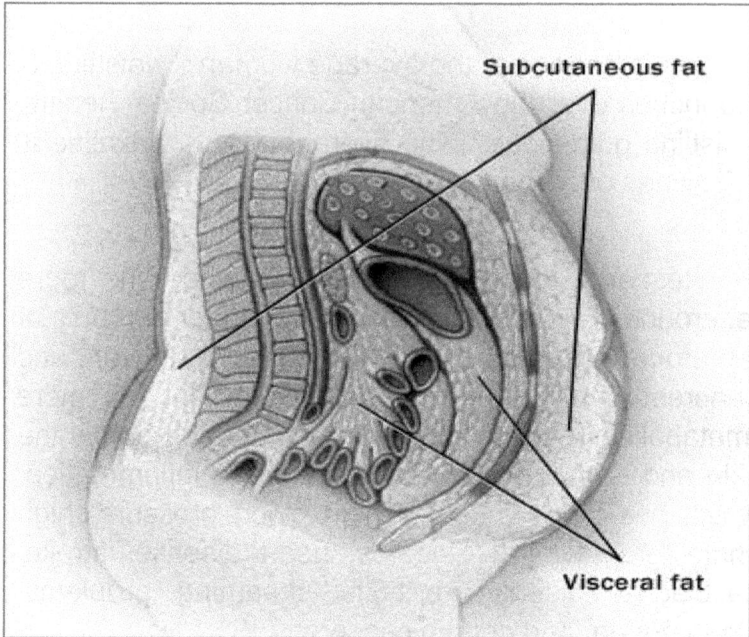

Source: He and She Fitness

Remember, for every five pounds you lose following The 21 Health Laws of Leadership, it may be equal to about one inch off your waistline.

Here is another reason you should reduce your waistline:

Wider waistlines may mean shorter lifespans.

Researchers warn that having a big belly means big trouble when it comes to your health.

They analyzed data from 11 studies that included more than 600,000 people worldwide and found that people with large waist circumferences were at increased risk of dying younger and dying from conditions such as heart disease, lung problems, and cancer.

Men with waists of 43 inches or more had a 50 percent higher risk of death than those with waists less than 35 inches. This equated to a three-year lower life expectancy after age 40.

Women with waists of 37 inches or more had an 80 percent higher risk of death than those with waists of 27 inches or less, which equated to a five-year lower life expectancy after age 40.

In other words, the larger the waist, the greater the risk, researchers said. For every two inches of increased waist circumference, the risk of death increased seven percent in men and nine percent in women, according to the study published in *Mayo Clinic Proceedings*.

Although the review found an association between larger waist size and risk of death at a younger age, it didn't prove a cause-and-effect relationship.

The link between a big belly and increased risk of death was seen even among people whose body-mass index (BMI) was within the healthy range, the researchers found. BMI is an estimate of body fat based on height and weight.

"BMI is not a perfect measure," study lead author Dr. James Cerhan, an epidemiologist at the Mayo Clinic, said in a journal news release. "It doesn't discriminate lean mass from fat mass, and it also doesn't say anything about where your weight is located. We worry about that because extra fat in your belly has a metabolic profile that is associated with diseases such as diabetes and heart disease."

When assessing patients, doctors need to consider both waist size and BMI.

"The primary goal should be preventing both a high BMI and a large waist circumference," Cerhan further stated. "For those patients who have a large waist, trimming down even a few inches—through exercise and diet—could have important health benefits."

I remember reading an article about a prince from Saudi Arabia. He was 41 years old, a billionaire, and loved horse racing. His horse had just won the Kentucky Derby. The photo in the article showed him in the winner's circle—he was very heavy and his waistline appeared to be over 60 inches, which would be around 27 inches over the recommended waistline guidelines of 35 inches for men. Three months after winning the Kentucky Derby, he had a massive heart attack in his sleep and died. Think about it—young, wealthy, with reportedly $15 billion in the bank, and he had just won the Kentucky Derby. He had succeeded in business, but he failed with his health.

Did you get a chance to see the Body Worlds Beneath the Skin tour? If you didn't, it is a must see. They had a display entitled "Suicide by Fat." Let me tell you about it. The Suicide by Fat display was a guy who weighed over 300 pounds and died at the age of 50 from a massive heart attack. When he died, they shipped his body to a group of scientists to examine his body and find out what exactly was the cause of his death. When the scientists received his body, the first thing they did was cut his body in half and open it up. They found a pacemaker. Behind the pacemaker was an enlarged heart. Just below his heart, he had an enlarged liver—fatty liver disease. Just below his liver, he had an enlarged gallbladder. On the other side of his chest cavity, he had an enlarged spleen.

Below the enlarged spleen, he had an enlarged pancreas. He'd had two hips replacements and two knee replacements. *Beyond* arthritis. And he had the muscle mass of a person who weighed only 115 pounds. That's like trying to drive a 12-wheeler uphill with a Pinto engine, which is almost impossible.

The most amazing thing to me was the amount of fat around his waistline. They were able to grab about 10 inches of fat. Wow, that's a lot of fat. That's why they called this display "Suicide by Fat." And this could happen to you if you don't reduce your waistline.

So, ladies your waistline should be under how many inches to be healthy? _____

And, guys your waistline should be under how many inches to be healthy? _____

Awesome! Let's move on to The Second Health Law of Leadership.

"Your waistline dictates your lifeline; the smaller your waistline, the longer your lifeline."

Jerry L. Anderson

The Second Health Law of Leadership

Have a Healthy Breakfast!

I want you to have a healthy breakfast. This will make sure you are jumpstarting your day with a meal that will supply the nutrients to give you energy for maximum productivity. This sets the tone for healthy eating all day. Keep this meal low in fat.

Here is another reason you should have a healthy breakfast:

A healthy breakfast can help you lose weight and feel great!

Boost fiber, cut down on fat and sugar to stay fit and trim, experts say.

A healthy breakfast that includes high-fiber cereal, fruit and milk can help you lose weight and fend off diabetes, heart disease, and stroke, says an article in the *Harvard Men's Health Watch.*

The article noted that research suggests that people who eat breakfast are leaner than those who skip breakfast. One study found that people who did without breakfast were at four times greater risk of obesity compared with those who started the day off right.

High-fiber cereals are essential to the health benefits of breakfast. Cereals should have at least six grams of fiber per serving but should have less than ten grams of sugar per serving. Eat high-fiber cereal with nonfat milk and bananas, berries or apple slices, the article suggests.

Other healthy breakfast choices include whole-grain or pumpernickel breads and trans-fat free soft margarine or cholesterol-lowering spreads containing plant stanols. While you don't need to eliminate eggs altogether, it's best to limit them to the occasional brunch.

Other breakfast foods, such as bacon, hash browns, and croissants have far too much fat or salt and should be avoided, the researchers said.

Of course, taste has a lot to do with how well an individual sticks to a particular breakfast, so the experts suggest trying out different foods to find out which offers you the most enjoyable—and healthy—morning meal.

I remember training a former NBA basketball player who was 6' 10", and now he is a sales professional. I asked him, "Larry, what do you eat for breakfast before you see your clients?"

He said, "I have three donuts and a cup of coffee."

"Let's try something different," I said. "I want you to start your day off with 16 ounces of water, a bowl of oatmeal or whole grain cereal, two pieces of whole wheat toast, and if you're still hungry, have a couple pieces of fresh fruit." Do you know that in less than a week Larry told me his energy level was so high he felt like a WWF wrestler. "Jerry, I can sell anything now."

Let me share this with you. I was talking to a guy in the gym the morning that I was speaking at a leadership retreat. "I heard you speak four months ago at the Global Conference and I started implementing the Have a Healthy Breakfast health law," he said. "In 16 weeks, I've lost 20 pounds, increased my energy and feel great." Let me repeat that. He lost 20 pounds which is four inches off his waistline, his energy increased, and he feels great.

These are the kind of results you can expect when you have a healthy breakfast.

So, my question to you is, are you going to go have a healthy breakfast, Yes or No?

Awesome! Let's move to The Third Health Law of Leadership.

"You should have a healthy breakfast every morning; it is the foundation of making healthy food choices throughout the day."

The Third Health Law of Leadership

Plan Your Workouts and Add Value!

I want you to plan your workouts and add value. At the start of the week, I want you to set the days of the week and the time of day you are going to work out. I want you to stick to it like you would to any other appointment with your doctor or dentist. You don't miss your doctor's appointment, you don't miss your dentist appointments, and I know you don't miss your appointments with your clients.

What I mean by *add value* is look at it this way. When you start exercising, it will take you off the list of heart disease, stroke, diabetes, high blood pressure, high cholesterol, being overweight, and obese. When you don't exercise, you are back on the list.

Here is another reason you should plan your workouts and add value:

Exercising removes you from all those health problems.

How important is exercise for my heart?

You may not care about increasing your strength. Firm, sexy abs may be the last thing on your mind. Fine. But even if you don't know your biceps from your bicuspids, there's one muscle you should never ignore: your heart.

Other muscles just get small and flabby when they aren't used. Your heart, on the other hand, might stop working. According to the American Heart Association (AHA), physical inactivity is a major risk factor for developing heart disease. The good news is that even moderate exercise, such as brisk walking, can make a big difference if done regularly. One study of healthy people over age 65 showed that those who exercised four to five times a week during their lifetimes had about 54 percent of the heart benefits seen in "master" athletes.

Exercise is also important if you have a chronic illness, such as diabetes, that's often accompanied by heart trouble. People with diabetes are two to four times more likely to develop cardiovascular disease, according to AHA. If you want to avoid heart disease— or you're recovering from heart trouble—a little sweat can work wonders.

I've been a couch potato all my life—isn't it too late to start exercising?

No, that's just one more reason to get moving. Even if you've already had a heart attack, a little exercise could save your life. A study published in the medical journal, *Circulation,* found that heart attack survivors who increased their activity levels were 90 percent more likely than inactive patients to be alive seven years after the attack!

How does exercise protect the heart?

Like any other muscle, the heart gets stronger with exercise. If you work out regularly, your heart muscle will grow a little larger and stronger, allowing it to move more blood with each beat. As a result, it takes fewer beats to get you through the day. Your heart rate drops, and your heart will enjoy a well-deserved rest.

Even more important, exercise helps protect your arteries—where heart attacks get their start. Regular exercise removes LDL ("bad") cholesterol from your blood. If you have too much of this fatty substance, it starts sticking to the walls of your arteries, causing arteriosclerosis, or hardening of the arteries. If the arteries feeding the heart become clogged—a condition called coronary heart disease—a heart attack may be just around the corner. The protection doesn't stop there. Exercise also increases your level of HDL ("good") cholesterol, a substance that helps keep your arteries clear.

In fact, your goal should be to make regular exercise a permanent part of your life. Besides being good for your heart, exercise has numerous other benefits, such as reducing stress, building strength and endurance, and helping prevent osteoporosis or bone thinning. Regular workouts can also lower high blood pressure and prevent type 2 diabetes, a condition that greatly raises the risk of heart trouble.

What kind of exercise is best?

You don't have to live at the gym to protect your heart. The AHA updated its guidelines on exercise in 2007, and now recommends at least 30 minutes of moderate exercise (like brisk walking) five days a week, or 25 minutes of vigorous exercise on at least three days in a week. In addition, they recommend that adults lift weights or do other muscular strength and endurance exercises at least twice a week. (If you need to lower your blood pressure or cholesterol, up that workout to forty minutes at least three or four times a week.)

After getting the go-ahead from your doctor, exercise to the point that you break a sweat or feel yourself short of breath. Start with as little as five minutes of exercise, which just about anyone can do, and build it into your daily routine. For example, you might start by taking a five-minute daily walk at lunchtime, or walking up and down a staircase for five minutes at a time. Try increasing the amount you exercise by a few minutes each week until you reach your target; realistic goals make it easier to succeed. The reward: unlike the stock market, exercise will give back everything you invest in it, with some benefits that are almost immediate.

Vigorous exercise—aerobic dancing, cycling, uphill hiking, swimming, and jumping rope—will definitely condition the heart and lungs. Stop-and-go activities like basketball, tennis, and soccer can help condition them as well. Interestingly, aerobic activities that involve the upper arms seem to offer more protection than other types. If you don't like rowing, swimming, or team sports, your best bet for heart protection is probably brisk walking. You can start anytime, and best of all, it's completely free.

But remember, any activity is better than nothing. You can give your heart a boost simply by working in the garden, getting up to change the channel instead of using the remote, doing chores around the house, and taking the stairs instead of the elevator. Do you know people who drive two blocks to mail a letter or buy a carton of milk? Don't be one of them. Put away your car keys during the day and do your errands on foot whenever possible.

If I'm a construction worker, do I still need to exercise?

Yes. It's a common myth that people who have non-sedentary jobs get enough exercise. They may do a lot of walking around, but it is usually not sustained. You need at least 15 to 20 minutes of uninterrupted exercise to get the metabolic benefits.

Is it safe for me to exercise?

If you're overweight or have been sedentary for a while, you'll want to get back into exercising gradually. In addition, you should have a thorough checkup before starting an exercise program.

Ask your doctor what heart rates you should target while exercising, especially if you're over 50, are pregnant, or have a condition that might make it difficult for you to exercise. Once you get the go-ahead, start slowly. Drink lots of water, including a glass before and after exercising, and keep a water bottle with you at all times. Keeping the body supplied with plenty of water helps prevent heat exhaustion and dehydration. See a doctor immediately if you feel light-headed, disoriented, faint, or experience chest pain, dizziness, and nausea.

Also, avoid being a "weekend warrior." If you're sedentary all week—that is, staring at a monitor or being a couch potato—don't go full blast on the weekends to make up. Not only is it a good way to get injured, but older, infrequent exercisers who work out too vigorously may even risk a heart attack. Any exercise is better than none, but sedentary types should exercise moderately and check with their doctor before starting a workout regime.

Not every heart, in fact, can handle all the rigors of exercise. If you have heart disease, you should have a thorough checkup before starting an exercise program, even if you just want to walk around the block. If you have heart pains or experience shortness of breath after a walk up the stairs, your doctor may want to give you a stress test, an exam that monitors your heart while you walk on a treadmill or ride a stationary bicycle.

The good news is that most people with heart disease can continue to lead an active life. As soon as you get your doctor's okay, you can start reaping the benefits of exercise. You'll feel stronger, more energetic, and less stressed. And one important muscle will be especially grateful.

I was speaking at a pastors' leadership conference, and a man approached me. "I used to work out every morning, but I don't anymore, and I feel great."

"Well, let me ask you a few questions," I said. "When you were working out every morning, how much did you weigh?" He said 185 pounds, then I asked him how much he weighed now. "235 pounds," he replied. Then I asked him, "When you were working out, did you have high blood pressure?" No. Then I asked, "Do you have high blood pressure now?" He said yes. "When you were working out, did you have high cholesterol?"

"No, but I do now," he said, and you could see a light switch turning on. "Are you diabetic now?" I asked. "Yes," he said, and stopped me from questioning him further. "Brother Jerry, my morning workout was helping me more than I thought." He didn't think it made any difference if he exercised or not, but look at the health problems he had after he stopped.

Let me share this with you. A guy talked to me at a leadership conference that he'd recently lost 60 pounds, and I congratulated him. "How'd you do it?" I asked. "I started working out every morning and a year later, here I am." We started discussing the benefits of losing weight when he added, "The discipline I used to lose the weight carried over into my business, and that's when I made my first million dollars." Did you hear what he said? I'm not promising you a million dollars when you plan your workout and add value, but I'm promising that you will become more productive.

At a leadership retreat, a woman came up to me and expressed her frustration in gaining weight over the last six months. "I don't know what to do," she said. "Every time I'm working out, my clients call and interrupt me." I told her the obvious, to just turn her cell phone off. "If I do that, I'm going to lose money," she said, frustrated.

"But working out regularly will probably add ten years to your life," I replied. "So how much money do you make a year?" "$300,000," she indicated. "Let's do the math," I offered. "If you make $300,000 a year and exercise is going to extend your life span by around 10 years, how much money are you going to make?" She paused a second, then said, "$3 million dollars." "Are you going to lose money?" She chuckled, "No." With that, I asked, "Should you exercise?" We both laughed.

A few months later, I picked up the phone to call a client I hadn't seen in the gym lately. "Are you working out somewhere else?" I asked her. "I'm so busy making money, I don't have time to work out," she told me. "Look, moneybags," I said. "You're making the dough but losing your health. You need to work out!" "I can't," she said in self-defeat. "Tell you what," I said. "I'll meet you at the gym Monday, Wednesday and Friday at 4 p.m. "I can't make it!" she told me emphatically. So I offered this deal, "Every day you show up, I'll give you $500." She laughed. "Okay, I'll be there," and she was. My point is when you add enough value, you will find a way to work out.

After relating this story to one of the anchors at CNN, she said, "Jerry, if you pay me to workout, I'll do it too." I thought for a second, and replied back, "You do get paid to work out by saving on healthcare costs. Look at it this way, a heart attack costs around $39,000, a stroke is around $35,000, and being diabetic is $6,000 a year."

So my question to you is, are you going to plan your workouts and add value, Yes or No?

Awesome! Let's move to The Fourth Health Law of Leadership.

"You should build exercise into your daily schedule; it should be part of your daily to-do list."

Jerry L. Anderson

The Fourth Health Law of Leadership

Skip the Soft Drinks!

I want you to skip the soft drinks and drink more water. Here's the reason. Your body loses ten glasses of water daily through normal bodily functions, and water is your most important nutrient. It delivers blood, oxygen, and nutrients to your cells. It removes waste from your cells and helps regulate your body temperature. I want you to drink at least ten glasses of water a day to keep your body hydrated. Here's an easy way to do it: drink 16 ounces of water before every meal. Think about this, too: if you decrease your soda intake by 200 calories a day, you'll have a 20-pound weight loss in one year. This equals to around four inches off your waistline.

**_Here is another reason you should
skip the soft drinks:_**

Sweetened drinks may damage your heart.

Soft drinks and other sugar-sweetened beverages can seriously damage heart health, a new review finds. The added sugar in sodas, fruit drinks, sweet teas, and energy drinks affects the body in ways that increase the risk of heart attack, heart disease, and stroke, it said.

Consuming one or two servings a day of sugar-sweetened beverages has been linked to a 35 percent greater risk of heart attack or fatal heart disease, a 16 percent increased risk of stroke, and as much as a 26 percent increased risk of developing type 2 diabetes, the report concluded.

Researchers say it's not going to solve the heart disease epidemic, but it's one way to have a measurable impact on your health.

The report published in the *Journal of the American College of Cardiology* is part of a new focus on excess sugar as a risk for heart disease, said Marina Chaparro, a clinical dietitian and spokeswoman for the Academy of Nutrition and Dietetics at Joe DiMaggio Children's Hospital in Hollywood, FL.

"Previously, everything focused on low fat, and reducing fat and cholesterol," said Chaparro. "The dietary guidelines that are about to come out really focus on added sugars and not as much on cholesterol and total fat. Those are important, but the impact of sugar has become much more profound."

Sugar-sweetened beverages account for about one-half of added sugars in the U.S. diet. One can of regular soda contains about 35 grams of sugar, which is equal to nearly nine teaspoons!

Manufacturers most often use either table sugar or high-fructose corn syrup to sweeten beverages. Both sugar sources contain roughly equal parts of two simple sugars, fructose, and glucose.

Researchers believe both fructose and glucose damage the heart. Glucose spikes blood glucose and causes insulin levels to rise, which can lead to the development of type 2 diabetes, Malik said. Diabetes is a risk factor for heart disease.

Fructose also causes heart health issues but in more insidious ways. Its presence can prompt the liver to release triglycerides and "bad" LDL cholesterol into the bloodstream. Too much fructose can lead to fatty liver disease.

Overconsumption of fructose can also lead to too much uric acid in the blood, which is associated with a greater risk of gout, a painful inflammatory arthritis.

48

Inflammation has also been linked to heart disease. Finally, fructose has been shown to promote the accumulation of belly fat, another risk factor for heart disease, researchers noted.

In all fairness, let's look at it from another angle. William Dermody Jr., vice president of policy for the American Beverage Association, said the new report unfairly knocks soda and sweet drinks.

"Here again is a study that in no way proves sweetened beverages uniquely cause illness, yet attempts to suggest it nonetheless," Dermody said. "There is no difference between sugar inherent to a product and sugar added to a product as far as the body is concerned. In both cases, the body metabolizes both the same way. This study's attempt to 'link' beverages to disease cannot overcome that well-grounded scientific finding."

But researchers are concerned that the liquid sugars in sweetened beverages might have a stronger impact on the body. "The fact it's in liquid form is something that's really of concern, because the sugars are absorbed really rapidly," Malik said. "They enter the bloodstream very quickly."

Either way for this argument, for now, researchers urge consumers to reduce the amount of added sugar in their diet. Limiting or eliminating sugar-sweetened beverages is a solid first step because many foods also contain added sugar.

The U.S. Department of Agriculture has proposed a new Nutrition Facts label that will identify the amount of sugar added to a product versus the amount that occurs naturally in the food, Chaparro and Malik said.

For example, a container of yogurt might note that nine grams of sugar come from the milk in the product, but that another ten grams of sugar have been added to make the yogurt even sweeter. Until the new label is available, consumers can avoid added sugars by paying close attention to the current Nutrition Facts label—which does list total sugars—and by scanning the list of ingredients for dextrose, sucrose, molasses, sugar, syrup or high-fructose corn syrup. If any of those are listed, you know that it's added sugar.

A woman contacted me asking for my help to lose 100 pounds. "How did you gain those 100 pounds?" I said. "I became really depressed when I broke up with my boyfriend and started drinking two liters of soda a day. I went from weighing 145 pounds to 245 pounds in just one year."

I'm telling you soda is a weight-gain product. It dumps all the sugar in your blood stream all at once and then you're hungry again because your stomach is empty. On the other hand, natural sugar puts glucose in your blood stream slowly, so your body can handle it properly and it keeps your stomach full.

I saw a lady on television the other day who said she drank three liters of soda a day and guest what? She's about 300 pounds overweight. She mentioned she only eats once a day though. She goes to the buffet every day at 12:00 noon and leaves at 9 p.m. Was this a joke? A nine-hour meal, and within that time frame she drinks over three liters of soda, which is about 4500 calories. It takes 3500 calories in excess of a 2500-calorie diet to gain one pound, so she is gaining about one pound a day drinking three liters of soda a day. Did she start out drinking three liters of soda a day? No, she started just like a lot of you, one can to two cans to three cans.

Listen to this, if you skip two 22-ounce soft drinks a day and replace them with two 22-ounce bottles of water, in one year you will have a 50-pound weight loss, which is about ten inches off your waistline.

My question to you is, are you going to skip the soft drinks and drink more water, Yes or No?

Jerry L. Anderson

Awesome! Let's move to The Fifth Health Law of Leadership.

"If you skip two sodas a day and replace them with two bottles of water and don't increase your caloric intake, in one year, you will have a 50-pound weight loss, which is about ten inches off your waistline."

The Fifth Health Law of Leadership

Have a 7 & 7 In The Morning!

I'm not talking about the mixed alcoholic drink. Whenever you don't have time to work out, I want you to have a 7 & 7 in the morning. This is made up of seven pushups and seven squats. This will keep your exercise habit in place when you don't have time to work out. It only takes about 30 seconds to do. Just stop, drop, and roll. Do seven pushups and seven squats. Take a shower, get dressed, and go to work. You're probably thinking, Jerry, how is this going to help me? Think about it, if you have a 7 & 7 every morning, its equal to 49 push-ups and 49 squats a week. This works out to be about 200 push-ups and 200 squats a month. That's 2400 push-ups and 2400 squats a year. Do you think this won't get you get in better shape? It will. The 7 & 7 is the fastest workout and the goal is to create the habit. Then create progression. With this strategy, I have seen so many people develop a daily exercise habit.

Here is another reason you should have a 7 & 7

in the morning:

Calistenics burns fat in two ways.

Calisthenics (exercising with your own bodyweight) tackle the problem of burning excess fat from two directions. First, the strength training builds muscle mass and tone all over your body. Increased muscle mass raises your resting metabolic rate, allowing you to burn more calories every moment of every day.

While specific spot training is impossible, short burst anaerobic exercises may just be your ticket to a trimmer belly. This style of training reduces subcutaneous and abdominal belly fat more effectively than other types of exercise, according to the *Journal of Obesity*.

British Journal of Nutrition also found that those who had exercised in a fasted state burned almost 20 percent more fat compared to those who had consumed breakfast before their workout. This means that performing exercise on an empty stomach provides the most desirable outcome for fat loss.

I was speaking at a women's conference and one woman told me she didn't have time to work out because she has two kids, plus she works fulltime. I told her in the morning to do seven pushups on the wall, grab the door handle and do seven squats, then take a shower and go to work. She called me back six weeks later. "Jerry, I have been having a 7 & 7 every morning for the last six weeks and lost twelve pounds. Now I'm up to a 21 & 21. A 12-pound weight loss is two and one-half inches off your waistline.

I remember talking to Gene who runs the control room at CNN. He told me he doesn't have time to work out because he needs to be at work at 4:00 in the morning. I had Gene do a 7 & 7 right in the control room which only took him 30 seconds. Three months later, I went back to CNN. Gene is up to a 50 & 50! First, you build the habit, then you create progression.

So my question to you is, are you going to have a 7 & 7 in the morning, Yes or No?

Awesome! Let's move to The Sixth Health Law of Leadership.

"If your team, congregation, or family knows you work out every morning and they see that you are energized and focused all day, you, as a leader, have done your job of being a great example for them."

The Sixth Health Law of Leadership

Trim the Fat!

I want you to trim the fat. Remove the skin and fat from meats before eating them. You are probably thinking, but fat is where the flavor is. No, I want you to use flavor for flavor, not fat for flavor. Think about it this way: if you remove eight ounces of fat from meat a week, that's about two pounds of fat a month and that's 24 pounds of fat a year, which is about five inches off your waistline. Over a 10-year time frame, you will have saved yourself 240 pounds of fat that could possibly clog and narrow your arteries.

Here is another reason you should trim the fat:

***Saturated Fat: Even a little splurge
may be too much.***

A fatty meal has an immediate, negative effect on heart health, research shows.

How bad can it be to indulge in an occasional meal or snack loaded with saturated fat? How about bad enough to diminish your body's ability to defend itself against heart disease?

A recent study by researchers at the University of Sydney in Australia found just that reaction after 14 trial participants, all healthy and between the ages of 18 and 40, ate just one piece of high-fat carrot cake and drank a milkshake.

That fat-laden feast compromised the ability of the participants' arteries to expand to increase blood flow. The sudden boost in what's known as saturated fat hampered the effects of so-called "good" cholesterol, the high-density lipoprotein or HDL, from doing its job–to protect the inner lining of the arteries from inflammatory agents that promote the build-up of fatty plaques. It's this plaque that, over time, clogs blood vessels and causes heart disease.

"Saturated-fat meals might predispose to inflammation of, and plaque buildup in, the vessels," the study leader, Dr. David Celermajer, pointed out, who is a Scandrett professor of cardiology at the Heart Research Institute and the Department of Cardiology at Royal Prince Alfred Hospital.

Celermajer's team had the volunteers eat two meals, spaced one month apart. Each meal consisted of a slice of carrot cake and a milkshake. But, in one case, the foods were made with saturated fat, and in the other case the meal was made with polyunsaturated safflower oil, a much healthier choice.

The high-fat meal, which contained about 90 percent saturated fat, had the equivalent of 68 grams of fat. In contrast, the meal made with polyunsaturated oil contained just 9 percent fat. The fat in the high-fat meal was equivalent to a 150-pound man or woman eating a double cheeseburger, a large order of french fries, and drinking a large milkshake.

Before and after each of the meals, the researchers obtained blood samples from the participants so they could evaluate whether the anti-inflammatory properties of the so-called good HDL cholesterol had decreased.

The anti-inflammatory properties did decrease after the saturated fat meal, the researchers said, but improved after the healthier polyunsaturated fat meal.

The effects may be temporary though. However, he's still concerned because the effect may be occurring over and over, each time a person eats a high-fat meal.

The message is clear what Celermajer said: It's important to limit saturated fat intake as much as possible. To do that, you first must know where saturated fat lurks, said Jeannie Moloo, a Sacramento, California, dietitian and a spokeswoman for the American Dietetic Association.

She suggests cutting down on meat, full-fat milk and other dairy products. Those foods are all major sources of saturated fat, Moloo said. So are processed foods and snacks.

Switching to low-fat or non-fat dairy products can minimize your total saturated fat intake. Choosing foods wisely by reading the Nutrition Facts label can help, too. For instance, an ounce of regular cheddar cheese contains 6 grams of saturated fat, while an ounce of part-skim mozzarella contains less than half that, or 2.9 grams.

Ice cream contains *a lot* of saturated fat, Moloo tells her patients. For instance, one cup of vanilla soft-serve ice cream has 13.5 grams of saturated fat. But some low-fat ice cream bars contain just 1.5 grams of saturated fat.

How much saturated fat per day is too much? Aim for 10 percent or less of your daily calories from saturated fat. The American Heart Association sets the bar for saturated fat at less than 7 percent of daily calories.

So, if your total calorie goal is 2,000 a day—reasonable for moderately active adults—you should aim for no more than 20 grams of saturated fat to keep your intake to 10 percent or so. While few people will take the time to add up their fat grams, doing so for a day or two can give you an idea of how you are doing.

I spoke at a church one year and they ended up asking me back the next year for their event. After my talk, one gentleman remarked how he'd used the Trim the Fat law and lost 37 pounds and seven inches from his waistline. "I didn't change what I eat, but now I trim the fat off of meats and remove the skin from chicken." This man had problems with his knees and hips before, but went on to say how he was virtually pain-free now. Pain can be the driver for staying away from exercise, but just by trimming the fat, you can reduce your bulk and alleviate strain on vital joints.

Interestingly, I came across some facts about high fat diets when doing some research for a CNN appearance. I happened to find the medical records of Dr. Robert C. Atkins, a man famous for the Atkins Diet that endorsed high fat and high protein. His medical records showed that upon his death, he was obese, had high blood pressure, high cholesterol, and atherosclerosis–the clogging and narrowing of the arteries, which had triggered multiple strokes. He died of a massive heart attack. If you try to pour fat down your sink, you know what's going to happen! The same thing will happen to your body if you follow a high fat diet.

I met another man who told me why he couldn't follow my Trim the Fat health law: because he loved chicken skin sandwiches. I outwardly cringed while he told me he fried a whole chicken, then took six pieces of chicken skin and put it between two slices of bread that had been spread with mayonnaise. Ew! That's a heart attack sandwich, but he claimed it was delicious. And we were at a health fair, if you can believe it!

But I must have gotten through to him because the next year when I saw him there, he looked like he'd lost weight. "You must've taken my advice," I joked, patting him on the shoulder. "Yes and no," he said. "My doctor checked my cholesterol and it was over 300. He wanted to put me on medication but I refused. I started not eating fat from meat and lost 40 pounds." He also said it took eight inches off his waistline and now his cholesterol is under 200 where it should be.

My question to you is, are you going to trim the fat, Yes or No?

Okay! We're ready to move on to The Seventh Health Law of Leadership.

"Carbohydrates have four calories per gram, proteins have four calories per gram, and fat has nine calories per gram. When you trim the fat, you can eat twice as much."

Jerry L. Anderson

The Seventh Health Law of Leadership

Pack Some Resistance!

Do you travel on a regular basis? If you do, I want you to pack some resistance. Travel with resistance bands. You can do a full body workout with your resistance bands in ten minutes. The reason I want you to pack some resistance is to help you keep your exercise habit in place when you travel.

Here is another reason you should pack some resistance:

Frequent business travel is tough on the heart.

American workers forced to travel often on business aren't doing their hearts any favor, a new study suggests.

A team of U.S. researchers found that people who travel for business 20 days or more per month are at higher risk for cardiovascular disease than light travelers who were on the go only a few days per month.

The team at Columbia University's Mailman School of Public Health analyzed the medical records of more than 13,000 people in a corporate wellness program. Nearly 80 percent of them were away from home overnight at least once a month and 1 percent were away from home nearly 20 days a month.

Compared with light travelers (who traveled 1 to 6 days a month), those who traveled 20 or more days a month had a higher body mass index, a lower level of "good" high density lipoprotein (HDL) cholesterol, and higher diastolic blood pressure. Diastolic pressure is the bottom number in a blood pressure reading.

Frequent travelers were also almost three times more likely to rate their health as being only "poor" to "fair," compared to people who were traveling less often.

Business travel by car, which leads to long hours behind the wheel, has also been linked by researchers for a higher likelihood of eating unhealthy foods. Workplace intervention programs and strategies can improve diet and activity though, a senior author of the study noted. It may surprise you to learn that vehicles in the U.S. are used 81 percent of the time for business travel, so it impacts a huge number of people.

When Arnold Schwarzenegger travels, he books the room next to him and turns it into a gym. Will Smith takes a van along with him that's full of gym equipment. These guys have deeper pockets than most of us, but what you can do is make sure the hotel you're staying in has gym facilities available to pack some resistance.

My question to you is, are you going to Pack Some Resistance when you travel, Yes or No?

Awesome! Let's move to The Eighth Health Law of Leadership.

"When you travel, you should always work out because it will keep you mentally sharp, energized, and ready for your task."

The Eighth Health Law of Leadership

Scale Down Your Favorites!

Do you have a favorite food you like to eat that you know is not healthy for you? I want you to scale down your favorites by 50 percent. I'm not saying don't have it. Just cut it in half. Start using a dish or plate that is 50 percent smaller than you normally use with your favorite food. This small change is going to produce big results for you.

Here is another reason you should scale down your favorites:

Desserts can actually be addictive.

Part of the problem with desserts is that they have a highly emotional connection with humans and can actually be addictive, according to Dr. Nora Volkow, director of the National Institute on Drug Abuse. Sweet and fatty foods like pastries and ice cream trigger pleasure centers in the human brain, which can make you want to eat even when you're full and can cause you to crave eating them again and again. In that respect, unhealthy desserts carry emotional and mental impacts as well as physical effects. To cut down, it can be helpful to serve yourself smaller portions and choose naturally sweet foods like fresh fruits.

I remember getting ready for a bodybuilding contest, and I bought a pack of 48 Snickers. I allowed myself to have one every night. The key was that I built the Snickers into my nutrition plan, so that I still had a reduced calorie deficit that kept me burning fat every week. Using this method never made me feel deprived, and gave me peace of mind that I was still sticking to my nutrition program.

One woman I talked to had scaled down everything in her kitchen: the dishes, the plates, the glasses and all of her silverware. In one year, she lost 200 pounds! That's about 40 inches off her waistline for a woman who used to weigh over 400 pounds.

But here's your big benefit and take away. By scaling down your favorites, you will be cutting about 200-300 calories a day which will yield you about a 20-30 pound weight loss in one year. That's about four to five inches off your waistline. And it also helps control your blood sugar intake and reduce your chances of becoming a diabetic.

So my question to you is! Are you going to scale down your favorite foods, Yes or No?

Awesome! Let's move to The Ninth Health Law of Leadership.

"Don't satisfy your taste buds and ruin your health; instead, eat something healthy that will satisfy your taste buds."

Jerry L. Anderson

The Ninth Health Law of Leadership

Walk at Work!

I want you to walk at work. For every two hours that you are sitting at your desk, I want you to get up and walk around for at least five minutes. Here's the reason: it will energize you, improve your circulation, and increase your productivity.

Here is another reason you should walk at work:

Even a ten-minute stroll can restore blood flow.

Researchers report that even a ten-minute stroll can restore blood flow to legs affected by prolonged sitting. "Although the size of our sample was small, the effects and results we found were still profound," said study first-author Robert Restaino, a doctoral student at the University of Missouri, in Columbia, Missouri.

The findings were published recently in the journal *Experimental Physiology.* "The obvious take-home is that uninterrupted sitting and inactivity leads to microvascular dysfunction, and therefore is unhealthy," said Dr. William Gray, director of endovascular services at New York-Presbyterian Hospital-Columbia University Medical Center, in New York City. Gray noted that sitting for a long time has previously been linked to heart disease.

Restaino said the goal of his study was to "tease apart the impairments elicited by prolonged sitting."

To isolate the effects of lengthy stretches of sitting, Restaino and his colleagues had eleven young men engage in some "acute sitting" for six hours. The researchers measured the men's blood flow and a couple of other heart factors both before the sitting session and afterward.

To keep food from affecting the results, all of the men ate the same breakfast—a quesadilla with pineapple juice—two hours before their sitting episode. They had another meal four hours into the sitting. The study participants were not supposed to move their legs while they sat, and they were seated so their legs hung above the floor. They were allowed to read or use a computer.

Once their six-hour sitting ended and blood flow and other measurements were completed, the men each took a 10-minute walk. The investigators again performed all of the same measurements. The researchers found that sitting was bad. It reduced blood flow in two major leg arteries and the men's calves swelled by almost an inch on average.

After the stroll, which, based on step counters, was about 1,100 steps in 10 minutes, blood flow and other measures returned to pre-sitting levels.

Noting that this group of 11 men represented "healthy individuals," Restaino said that in other groups of people, such as the elderly or those with previous heart problems, "I would imagine the impairments would be more exaggerated." For people who are less healthy, the ability of blood flow and other measures to rebound to normal might require longer, more intense exercise. But "this is purely speculative" for now, Restaino said.

Researchers further stated that blood flow dysfunction can be associated with worse cardiovascular (heart and blood vessels) outcomes in older adults; however, it's unclear whether age or duration would have changed the effects seen in this study.

The direct effect of exercise appears to be increased levels of nitric oxide, a molecule that triggers blood vessels to open up. That reduces friction on the blood and allows it to flow more easily. The contraction of muscles while walking also helps to boost circulation.

Over all, short walks do play an important role with prolonged bouts of sitting.

A friend of mine said she sits at her desk eight hours a day and she was gaining weight, her energy level was low, and her feet were swelling. I suggested to her to walk for ten minutes in the morning, ten minutes at noon, and ten minutes in the afternoon. Do you know in six months, she lost thirty pounds, increased her energy, and her feet stopped swelling!

At a leadership conference, a manager cornered me in the men's room and told me every three hours, he gets his sales team up and has them walk around the building. Then he noticed something. When they got back to their desks, they were all re-energized and they closed more deals. He went on to tell me in the last six months, he's lost 40 pounds and eight inches off his waistline walking with his team every three hours. Do you think he's going to stop that? Of course not! Walking at work will not only keep you healthy, but it will keep you wealthy.

So my question to you is, are you going to walk at work, Yes or No?

Awesome! Let's move to The Tenth Health Law of Leadership.

"Walking is one on the best ways to lower your blood sugar, increase your energy, and keep disease at bay."

Jerry L. Anderson

The Tenth Health Law of Leadership

Slow Down Your Eating Speed!

I want you to slow down your eating speed. This is how you can do it. I want you to take a bite every 30 seconds and then chew your food at least 20 times before swallowing. Make sure you put your spoon or fork down after every bite. This will help you stop swallowing and start chewing, which will prevent you from overeating. Because most people are tossing their food from their lips to their throat, never satiating their taste buds with or around the outside of your tongue.

Here is another reason you should slow down your eating speed:

Eating too quickly may raise your risk of diabetes.

Researchers from Lithuania compared 234 people with type 2 diabetes and 468 people without the disease and found that those who gobbled down their food were 2.5 times more likely to have diabetes than those who took their time while eating.

Study participants with diabetes also were more likely to have a higher BMI rate based on height and weight, and to have much lower levels of education than those without diabetes, the researchers said. "The prevalence of type 2 diabetes is increasing globally and becoming a world pandemic," study leader Lina Radzeviciene of the Lithuanian University of Health Sciences said in a European Society of Endocrinology news release. Also mentioned were genetic and environmental factors that might help people reduce their chances of developing the disease.

Although the study found an association between eating fast and the incidence of diabetes, it did not prove a cause-and-effect relationship.

After speaking at a conference, I sat down for lunch with some attendees. At my table, the guy across from me was eating so fast he ate three plates of food in less than ten minutes. He was sweating and breathing very heavily, and I don't think he realized it. I guessed that he was about 125 pounds overweight. I'd seen him earlier walk out the door during my speech. Maybe he didn't want to hear what I had to say, but he did return just before lunch.

The next time you're in a public place, such as a mall, notice in the food court who is eating fast and whether they're overweight or not. There's usually a direct correlation between the two. I've seen people eat so fast that I felt like giving them speeding tickets for going too fast in a loading zone!

So my question to you is, are you going to slow down your eating speed, Yes or No?

Awesome! Let's move to The Eleventh Health Law of Leadership.

"You should eat just enough for your particular type of work. If you work in an office, don't eat like a construction worker."

The Eleventh Health Law of Leadership

Build Your Muscles!

I want you to build your muscle and turn your bodies into fat burning machines by lifting weights at least two to three times a week. Think about this: the more muscle you have, the more calories you burn every hour of the day—even while you're sitting at your desk or watching television. It will also give you a more youthful appearance and the strength and stamina to go with it.

Here is another reason you should build your muscles:

Weight lifting helps you lose weight!

Frustrating as it may seem, banishing extra fat isn't impossible. Study after study has shown that the clincher after cutting back on calories is exercise. But as you charge into the gym, don't forget to enlist one of your best fat-fighting allies: your own muscles.

If you want to get into shape, aerobic workouts can't be beat for their power to tune up the heart and lungs. Aerobics will also tone the muscles you're using. But pumping iron can be another potent weapon in the battle against the bulge. Weight training will not only shore up your bones, build additional muscle mass, and make it easier to heft grocery bags or firewood, it can also help hold the line on your waistline.

Lose what you don't need.

If you're dieting, weight lifting can help you lose fat instead of muscle and bone. Most people don't realize it, but when they diet, only about 60 to 75 percent of the weight they lose is actually fat. So if you shed 20 pounds, five or six of those pounds are from nonfat tissue, including muscle, bone, and water, leaving your body weaker. But exercise, particularly the iron-pumping kind, can preserve muscle and bone, so that up to 85 percent of what you trim is fat, says Dale Schoeller, a nutrition researcher at the University of Wisconsin at Madison.

We all tend to fatten up as we get older, and one key culprit is the dwindling of muscle mass that begins in our 20s or 30s. After 40, we lose roughly a third of a pound of brawn a year. And since muscle burns more calories than fat does, our metabolism slows down. In women, who start out with proportionately less muscle than men, this process takes a bigger toll on the waistline. The average female gains around 20 to 25 pounds of fat between the ages of 20 and 50.

Weight training can also raise a person's metabolic rate for as long as 12 hours after exercising. That means that if you lift weights, your body will burn calories faster. But whether or not regular exercise generally increases your metabolism over the long-term remains controversial, says Glenn Gaesser, an exercise physiologist at the University of Virginia in Charlottesville.

One study in the Netherlands found that 18 weeks of weight training by young men sped up their metabolism by 9 percent. Other studies haven't found such a benefit. Nonetheless, Gaesser and others believe that by maintaining muscle, weight lifting can help minimize the metabolic downturn that occurs as you get older.

Here's the math: a pound of muscle burns five to ten calories daily, even if you're lying on the couch. With a moderately strenuous weight-lifting regimen, women can gain one to two pounds of muscle after three months; men rack up about twice as much. Two extra pounds of brawn would thus consume 10 to 20 calories daily. That seems like small change, but over months and years, it can really add up. "Ten calories a day is 3,650 calories a year, which is equivalent to about a pound of body fat," says Gaesser. Over 20 years, that extra bit of muscle could keep you from putting on 20 pounds. "So it can make a rather sizable difference in the long term."

Indeed, nutrition researcher Miriam Nelson, director of the Center for Physical Fitness at Tufts University, often sees weight lifting open the door to a trimmer body. In one study, she put 10 overweight women on the same diet, but half of them lifted heavy weights twice a week. Both groups ended up around 13 pounds lighter on the scale. But that wasn't the whole story. On average, the diet-only crew lost only 9.2 pounds of fat, whereas the lifters actually lost 14.6 pounds of fat and gained 1.4 pounds of muscle.

That points up a neat thing about strength training: You may not necessarily lose more weight, but you can still gradually slim down as you trade fat for brawn. Contrary to female fears, crunching dumbbells won't turn women into the Incredible Hulk. If anything, it'll make them smaller as they replace jiggly fat with compact muscle, says Nelson. Even more gratifying, people who pump iron notice striking improvements in strength fairly quickly, giving them more stamina for walking or biking. Two more major long-term bonuses, especially for older women: You increase muscle mass and you gain bone density.

A lot of us think as we get older, we get weaker and lose our strength and appearance. It's not true. I saw a great case of it at a bodybuilding contest. This contest had different categories for 40-, 50-, 60-, and 70-year-olds. Each person who won their category had a showdown for the best body in the contest. Lo and behold, the 70 year-old guy took first place. He had the best body in the contest. His abs were ripped! You have to remember, muscle adapts to stress, not to age, which is the SAID (Specific Adaptation on Imposed Demand) principle.

For instance, over 25 years ago, I worked at the Long Beach City College Human Performance Lab in charge of about 50 seniors. I put them on a full body strength training program three times a week, and the results were phenomenal. They all increased their strength by at least 300 percent. They were so thrilled about their results, they started strength training every day. I had to stop them, though, because you should only strength train every other day. They got so mad at me, I thought they were going to call the Senior Care Action Network (SCAN) and report me! The point is, your body will stay strong with strength training no matter how old you are. The body is a marvelous adaptability machine!

To look at this another way, one of my clients asked me to train his wife because she was under weight and too skinny. Four months after we started, he called me up. "I thought you were going to put some weight on her," he said sternly. "She looks like she's getting smaller and losing weight." I asked him to stop by at our next training session and I'd show him some things. Together, all three of us looked at her weight chart. It showed she'd started out at 112 pounds. Now she weighed 127 pounds, but had lost three inches off her waistline. He was shocked, but muscle takes up less space than fat and that's what made her look smaller. So ladies, don't be afraid of weight training. It will tone you up and reduce inches from your waistline.

Let me share this story with you. It's a little long but worth reading. I was telling one of my clients the other day, "Jackie, you're doing great on your program." She'd lost 40 pounds (eight inches off her waistline) and increased her strength drastically. She could bench press 95 pounds, squat 165 pounds, and curl 25-pound dumbbells in each hand. She had more curves than the Long Beach Grand Prix auto race! One day she came to the workout and told me, "I think I'm as strong as you said I was." "How'd you find out?" I asked and laughed.

"Last night," she said, "my boyfriend was watching the basketball game and during the commercials, he was doing curls with his dumbbells. I asked him how much they weighed. He told me not to try and lift them for fear I'd hurt myself. "These are 15 pounds," he told me. "These are too heavy for you." "I do 25 pounds when I'm at the gym," I informed him.

"Are you saying you're stronger than me?" he challenged. He got a little upset and said, "Okay, let's arm wrestle and I will prove to you that I'm stronger than you." So we arm-wrestled and guess what happened? I beat him! Then I beat him again the second time!"

"Did you use one hand or two?" I asked her, curious that she might have had an unfair advantage. "Just one hand," she said. "Then he tried to wrestle me down and pull one of those MMA submission holds on me. I pinned him and he couldn't get up. Then we tried it again, and I pinned him a second time." We had a good laugh afterwards. Ladies, I'm not recommending that you lift weights so you can pin your man. But if you stay strong, the choice is yours!

I trained a sales professional who wanted to build muscle and lose weight. So I put him on a strength training workout three days a week. In a year, we increased his muscle mass and reduced his body fat percentage which noticeably changed his appearance. That's when his self-confidence and self-esteem improved, which, in turn, had a great impact on his productivity at work. His sales went from $500k to $1 million dollars the first year he trained with me. The next year his sales shot up to $3 million, then $5 million after the third year.

But here is your big takeaway and your big bonus: when you start building your muscles, in about six to eight weeks you will increase your lean muscle mass about five to ten pounds. Five pounds of muscle burns about twenty pounds of fat a year, which is about four inches off your waistline. And ten pounds of muscle burns about forty pounds of fat a year, which is about eight inches off your waistline.

Remember what I told you earlier, building your muscle will also give you a more youthful appearance and the strength and stamina to go with it.

My question to you is, are you going to build your muscles, Yes or No?

Awesome! Let's move to The Twelfth Health Law of Leadership.

"Your muscles are like your car engine; the more you have, the more fuel/calories you burn every hour of the day, even while you're sitting at your desk or watching television."

The Twelfth Health Law of Leadership

Supersize Your Salad at Lunch!

I want you to supersize your salad before you eat your lunch. Don't get one of those wimpy little salads and put unhealthy salad dressing on it. I want you to supersize it and put healthy salad dressing on it. Here's the reason: when you supersize your salad before you eat your lunch, it will provide all the nutrients that you need to keep you energized, alert, and productive in the afternoon. And this will prevent you from overeating and getting sluggish.

Here is another reason you should supersize your salad:

A salad before your meal may help reduce your total energy intake during that meal.

According to Michelle Cardel, PhD, RDA, in *Academy Today*, eating a salad before a meal can reduce your caloric intake during the meal and over the course of the entire day. This can be beneficial for weight loss and healthy weight management. Eating a salad first may also help boost vegetable consumption by 23 percent, according to another study published in *Appetite*.

This one guy was telling me he supersized his salad at lunch for a year and a half and lost 95 pounds. He went from weighing 280 pounds down to 185 pounds.

One of the anchors at CNN said to me, "If I supersize my salads, I won't be able to eat the cake!" Of course you won't! Because if you supersize your salad, your meal will probably be cut in half and you won't *want* to eat cake. But your benefit is that it will save you about 300 calories a day. If you cut your calories every day at lunch by 300 calories, you will have about a 30-pound weight loss in one year. That's about six inches off your waistline.

I was watching on TV an interview of a top sales producer, who earns a million dollars a year in commissions. He said at lunch he has a large salad with chicken on top every day. His reason being that he noticed when he had a large salad with chicken, he felt more energized and productive in the afternoon. Then he said something that really caught my attention. "Lunch is for ingesting healthy things into your body." Think about it, if a top producer who is earning a million dollars a year in commissions is supersizing his salad so that he can be more productive in the afternoon, what should you do? Copy from success.

So my question to you is: Are you going to supersize your salad before your lunch, Yes or No?

Awesome! Let's move to The Thirteenth Health Law of Leadership.

"Supersizing your salad at lunch will provide you with the nutrients you need to stay energized, alert, and productive in the afternoon."

The Thirteenth Health Law of Leadership

Get Active!

I want you to get active. Do you exercise three times a week? Do you exercise five times a week? Do you watch 30 minutes of television a day? Listen to this: I want you to do cardiovascular exercise at least five days a week and for at least 20 to 30 minutes per day. Here's an easy way to do it. Exercise while watching television. Every time you grab the remote and turn on the television, I want you to jump on the treadmill, lifecycle, or march in place for 10 to 30 minutes while you watch the tube. This will help you get your heart and lungs in shape and increase your calorie burning.

Here is another reason you should get active:

Why should i get active?

How can I make myself exercise when I'm so tired all the time?

Start out slowly. If you haven't been active in a while, see your doctor before starting an exercise program. Then try just walking for a few minutes each day. In the beginning, you may find that you're tired after a workout or that you have to force yourself to take a walk even though you'd rather take a nap. But if you can stick with it for a few weeks, you'll discover your energy increasing. If you don't, you should probably see your doctor. You may just be pushing too hard, not getting enough sleep, not eating enough calories, or not getting enough nutrients. But you'll also want to rule out any health problems.

How can exercise give me more energy?

One reason for the increase in energy is that aerobic exercise makes your heart stronger and more efficient. A fit cardiovascular system delivers about 25 percent more oxygen per minute at rest and 50 percent more oxygen during physical exertion than an unfit one does. Stronger muscles give you the endurance to get yourself through the day with energy to spare. Exercise can also improve the quality of your sleep, so you feel more rested even after spending the same amount of time in bed.

If my muscles are screaming and I'm gasping for breath in the first few minutes, should I keep going?

No. Slow down and catch your breath. Once you feel more comfortable you can start building up your pace slowly. Your muscles may hurt at first because they're burning carbohydrates without oxygen and producing a waste product called lactic acid that causes fatigue. If you've been spending a lot of time on the couch, your lungs aren't used to the need to boost their oxygen intake at a moment's notice. But once you've built up a little endurance, your breathing should catch up with your effort, giving your muscles the oxygen they need. The better the shape you're in, the sooner you'll reach this state of greater endurance. If you find you can't recover your breath after a few minutes, see your doctor. You could be suffering from exercise-induced asthma.

The "exercise high" phenomenon

When you exercise intensely, the stress on your body prompts your brain to release substances called endorphins into your bloodstream. These chemicals hook onto nerve receptors all over your body, blocking pain signals. They may cause you to feel euphoric—simultaneously relaxed and energized—even hours after you've stopped sweating. A leisurely walk around the block probably won't do the trick. Researchers say you have to work out at about 75 percent of your maximum heart rate for at least 30 minutes for endorphins to kick in. (You can find your maximum heart rate by subtracting your age from 220.) But any kind of regular activity will give you more energy on a day-to-day basis. You don't have to become addicted to endorphins to benefit.

I have to share this story with you. I remember speaking to a group of seniors and my audience was anywhere between 65 and 95 years old. After my presentation, one senior came up to me and was telling me what they did to exercise. And then I noticed something–this is an observation, not a study– all the seniors who told me they enjoyed exercising were all walking, and all the seniors who told me they didn't like to exercise and weren't going to do it, were all using walkers. Yes, your decision to exercise on a regular basis may determine whether you are going to be walking or using a walker when you get older. The choice is yours.

I have a buddy whose father was in a convalescent home. He had been on bed rest for the last two years. His father had diabetes, COPD, and a sore on the outside of his lower right leg that wouldn't heal. He was upset about the care his dad was receiving and took him home. When he got his father home, he told his dad to walk up the stairs in his house once a day. In seven days, the sore on his lower right leg went away. "I didn't expect that sore to heal when I asked him to walk up those steps every day," he said incredulously.

"The life of the creature is in the blood," I said. "Walking up the stairs in your house increased his blood flow in his lower body, and it brought fresh oxygen and nutrients into his cells and removed toxins from his cells," I explained. That's how he was healed. Because there's no circulation laying in a bed.

Even in Las Vegas, they are picking up on what I am asking you to do, which is to do two things at one time: exercise while watching television. Some of the casinos have attached the recumbent bike, the one you sit down on and pedal, to the slot machine. Yes! You can lose money and lose weight all at the same time! So now when you walk out of the casino, you are lighter in the wallet and smaller in the waistline!

I saw this story on television and they were interviewing this woman who was celebrating her 100th birthday. The reporter asked her, "What is the key to your long life?" She said, "I get up every morning and ride my lifecycle eight miles." Word to the wise!

So my question to you is, are you going to get active, Yes or No?

Awesome! Let's move to The Fourteenth Health Law of Leadership.

"If you close the door to exercise, you just opened the door to the hospital."

Jerry L. Anderson

The Fourteenth Health Law of Leadership

Weigh Yourself!

Have you weighed yourself this week? Have you weighed yourself this month?   Have you weighed yourself this year? Are you afraid to weigh yourself? I want you to weigh yourself every morning before you eat breakfast and write it down in your calendar. After a few weeks of following the 21 Health Laws of Leadership, you'll have a graph of your weight going down and your new trim waistline coming in. And if you start gaining weight, you can stop it before it gets out of control.

Some people say you should not weigh yourself. That's like saying don't check your gas gauge, don't check your bank account and don't check your email. The scale gives you information about what's going on with your body.

Here is another reason you should weigh yourself every day:

104

Daily weigh-ins keep dieters on track.

Checking your weight every day could help you slim down, researchers report. A two-year Cornell University study found that tracking the results of daily weight checks on a chart helped people lose weight and keep it off.

"You just need a bathroom scale and an Excel spreadsheet, or even a piece of graph paper," study senior author David Levitsky, a professor of nutrition and psychology said.

People who lost weight with this approach in the first year maintained that weight loss throughout the second year. That result is significant because previous studies have shown that about 40 percent of weight loss is regained within a year, and nearly 100 percent is regained within five years, so this is good news.

This approach compels you to be aware of the connection between your eating and your weight. "It used to be taught that you shouldn't weigh yourself daily, and this is just the reverse," he said.

While daily weight checks did help women, they had a much greater effect in men, although researchers aren't sure why.

At one of my speaking engagements, a man told me that he lost 40 pounds in 30 days. Alarmed by such a huge weight loss in such a short time period, I asked what type of diet he was on. "I wasn't on a diet," he said. "I got nervous after losing 10 pounds a week for three weeks in a row, and called my doctor." It ended up with his doctor diagnosing diabetes. Gaining weight is unhealthy to your body and losing weight quickly is unhealthy for your body, and like in this case, it could indicate illness. That's why it's very important to weigh yourself daily and record it. The scale gives you information about what's going on in your body.

My question to you is, are you going to weigh yourself, Yes or No?

Awesome! Let's move to The Fifteenth Health Law of Leadership.

"You should make the scale your friend, control it, don't let it control you! It's only a guide to help you get to a healthy waistline."

The Fifteenth Health Law of Leadership

Stay Positive!

I want you to take five minutes in every day and read or listen to something positive. You have to train your mind to be positive. It's not going to happen on its own. This will help you stay mentally fit so you can follow the 21 Health Laws of Leadership. You can listen to a positive message while you're getting ready for work in the morning, in the car, or while exercising. The bottom line is it needs to done daily.

Here is another reason you should stay positive:

Longer life spans, less stress, increased resistance to the common cold and more!

According to the Mayo Clinic, positive thinking is linked to a wide range of health benefits including: longer life spans, less stress, lower rates of depression, increased resistance to the common cold, better stress management and coping skills, lower risk of cardiovascular, disease-related death, increased physical well-being, and better psychological health.

I have trained many champion athletes and they all have one thing in common: they stayed mentally fit by adopting the championship mindset to stay positive. On the other side of the coin, I have trained many athletes who should have been champions and they also had one thing in common: they didn't stay positive and let everything but their goal become their main focus.

I was training this one guy for a contest, and all he did was complain. One day he came in and started in, so I told him, "Go get on the lifecycle and warm up for 15 minutes, and get your attitude together or just go home." He came back for his workout with a new attitude and had a great workout. During his workout, he took his sweatshirt off and looked in the mirror in shock. "When I came to the gym today," he said incredulously, "I went into the locker room, took off my shirt, and I caught a glimpse of myself in the mirror. I looked terrible. Look at me now," he beamed. "I look great!"

Funny, but when you change your attitude, it changes your entire appearance, your stance— everything. Remember that your mind tells your body what to do.

My question to you is, are you going to stay mentally fit, Yes or No?

Awesome! Let's move to The Sixteenth Health Law of Leadership.

"Your mind is the only thing that can stop your body from becoming healthy."

Jerry L. Anderson

The Sixteenth Health Law of Leadership

Eat More Fruits and Vegetables!

Do you eat at least three servings of fruit and vegetables a day? Do you eat at least five servings of fruit and vegetables a day? You should eat a minimum of five servings of fruit and vegetables every day. Fruit and vegetables provide the vitamins, minerals, and fiber to help nourish your body properly. They are your leader nutrients; they protect your health and fight off disease. And they are low in fat, sodium, and cholesterol.

Here is another reason you should eat more fruits and vegetables:

Reduction in risk of heart disease, stroke, cardiovascular disease, cancer, and premature death.

If you want to add years to your life, ten daily servings of fruits and vegetables may be the best recipe you can follow, an analysis suggests.

The benefits show up in lower rates of heart attack, stroke, cancer, and early death. If everyone found a way to get 10 daily servings of produce, 7.8 million deaths would be avoided each year worldwide.

It may seem like a lot because this equates to ten small bananas or apples a day, but you can also receive the benefits in spinach, peas, broccoli or cauliflower, which means about thirty tablespoons per day. If you can't do ten a day, try for five servings because that's what is currently recommended by many health agencies.

Even over two portions a day made a difference in the review. Eating 2.5 portions of produce on a daily basis was associated with reductions in: heart disease (16 percent), stroke (18 percent), cardiovascular disease (13 percent), cancer risk (4 percent), and premature death (15 percent).

However, the results of 10 daily servings is much stronger with a 24 percent reduction risk of heart disease, a 33 percent reduced risk of stroke, a 28 percent reduced risk of cardiovascular disease, 13 percent reduced risk of cancer, and a 31 percent reduction in premature death risk. They also reduce cholesterol levels, blood pressure; and they boost the health of our blood vessels and immune system. The complex network of nutrients they hold contain many antioxidants, which may reduce DNA damage and lead to a reduction in cancer risk. But no cause and effect relationship was found in longer life spans.

These facts about fruits and vegetables are based on the analyses of 95 studies involving almost 2 million people!

In their review, the researchers also found signs that the following types of produce seemed to garner the greatest benefits: apples, pears, citrus fruits, green leafy vegetables, cruciferous vegetables (such as broccoli, cabbage and cauliflower), and green and yellow vegetables (such as green beans, spinach, carrots and peppers).

I remember reading an article about Ruben Studdard, the second season winner on American Idol. After American Idol, he gained 100 pounds. He was already a big guy weighing in at 355 pounds while filming the show. One day he looked in the mirror and said to himself, "I need to do a better job at taking care of my body." The next day he started eating fruits, vegetables, and grains. In one year, he lost over 100 pounds. I recently saw him on the Biggest Loser show. He had stopped eating fruits and vegetables and gained all the weight back and more.

A lot of people tell me, "Jerry, eating five servings of fruits and vegetables a day is a lot." But I see that same person eating a double cheese burger, large fries, apple pie, and a large coke. Go figure!

This guy at the gym told me his doctor said he needed to lose weight for his health and he asked me what to do. "Start eating six pieces of fruit and six servings of vegetables a day." He said he couldn't do it. I then advised him to eat three pieces of fruit on the way to work, three pieces on his way home, and eat vegetables at lunch and dinner. I saw him three months later, and he told me he'd lost thirty pounds and six inches off his waistline. It was that easy!

So my question to you is, are you going to eat more fruit and vegetables, Yes or No?

Awesome! Let's move to The Seventeenth Health Law of Leadership.

"As your fruit and vegetable intake goes up, your waistline will go down; as your fruit and vegetable intake goes down, your waistline will go up."

The Seventeenth Health Law of Leadership

Track Your Fiber!

I want you to track your fiber daily. Most people eat less than 10 grams of fiber a day. I want you to eat at least 25 grams of fiber a day. Here is the reason. The higher the fiber content in your diet, the lower your body weight will be. This will help you achieve your healthy waistline goal with no problems. Remember, real food has fiber.

Here is another reason you should track your fiber:

Fiber is the Rx for disease-free aging.

An Australian study found that not only can foods rich in fiber keep you "regular," they may help you live longer without disease. Fiber-rich foods include fruits and whole grains.

Although this was a small study, colleagues weren't surprised by the findings, "given that there are numerous studies showing fiber's protective influence against a host of chronic diseases."

"Successful aging" was defined in the study as the continued absence of physical disability, depression, breathing problems, or chronic health issues such as cancer, high blood pressure, diabetes, or heart disease.

"People can achieve the recommended intake of fiber consumption—around 30 grams per day—by eating a wide range of foods such as whole-grain breads and cereals, fruits, vegetables and legumes," Gopinath, associate professor in the University of Sydney's Westmead Institute for Medical Research noted.

The researchers tracked the study participants, who were 49 years and older, for a decade starting in 1994. At the start, all were free of cancer and heart disease. When the study concluded, 15.5 percent of the participants had aged successfully over the 10-year time frame. By contrast, those whose fiber consumption was pegged at below-average levels were least likely to have aged well.

The researchers also found that only 25 percent of study participants were meeting daily fiber intake recommendations. This accurately reflects general population habits. Certain fruits and vegetables contain more fiber than others, like nuts, seeds, beans, avocados, strawberries, raspberries, blueberries, oranges, carrots, leafy greens, corn, peas, popcorn, bran cereals, and oatmeal.

But what exactly is it about fiber that promotes longevity? "Based on our study we can't exactly pinpoint as to how fiber influences aging status," one of the researchers said. But the team speculates that fiber may affect blood sugar levels and minimizing inflammation throughout the body.

For one thing, not all fiber is the same. Soluble and insoluble dietary fiber have different functions in the body.

I talked to one of my clients about the Importance of tracking his fiber. The next day he came to the workout with a fiber counting book, and started eating only foods that were high in fiber. He carried that book around with him everywhere; he checked the fiber in every food before he ate. In six months, his weight went from 225 to 185. He lost 40 pounds and eight inches off his waistline in six months. Previously he was considered pre-diabetic, had high blood pressure, and high cholesterol. After losing the weight, all his health issues were gone. This is the result of the power of focusing on fiber daily.

I remember watching the sales manager at the health club (Yes, the health club!) eating fried chicken, pizza, and hamburgers every afternoon. He had his whole team doing it. He'd gained 70 pounds in one year and went from being the number one salesmen to the bottom. One of his salesmen, Frank, was my client. "Don't eat that stuff," I told him. "Focus on fiber." The sales manager gained seventy pounds, ruined his image and he wasn't believable anymore. Guest what? After our talk, Frank lost 35 pounds focusing on fiber and the company promoted him to sales manager.

Listen to this: when you start tracking your fiber, you will probably reduce your daily calorie intake about 300 to 500 calories a day, which will be about a 30 to 50-pound weight loss in one year. That's about six to ten inches off your waistline.

So my question to you is, are you going to focus on fiber, Yes or No?

Awesome! Let's move to The Eighteenth Health Law of Leadership.

"High fiber foods will keep your stomach full; they put the nutrients in your bloodstream slowly, and help to control the emotional side of eating."

The Eighteenth Health Law of Leadership

Avoid Fad Diets!

I want you to avoid fad diets. There are over 30,000 diets on the market and 75 percent of men and 67 percent of women are overweight or obese. Fad diets don't work. Let me make it simple for you. Any diet that does not have the six nutrients that your body needs daily to function properly (protein, carbohydrates, fat, vitamins, minerals, and water) is unhealthy for you. There are no shortcuts to losing weight or reducing your waistline.

Here is another reason you should avoid fad diets:

Fad diets are dangerous.

They're potentially dangerous and ultimately ineffective. That's the advice of the American College of Preventive Medicine (ACPM), a physician group whose members are dedicated to health promotion and disease prevention. Forget fad diets for weight control.

This group issued a policy statement voicing strong opposition to any weight-loss approach that fails to take overall health into account. The group warns against fad diets, and is especially critical–without expressly naming it–of the Atkins Diet, the low-carbohydrate, high-fat eating plan that has attracted legions of followers, although the spokesperson for that organization took issue with this statement.

The ACPM statement was in response to the growing epidemic of obesity and type 2 diabetes in the United States. More than 97 million American adults are overweight, with a body mass index (BMI) of 25 or higher. A 5-foot-5 woman who weighs 150 pounds and a 6-foot-tall man who weighs 185 pounds, each has a BMI of 25, for instance. Excess weight boosts the risk of heart disease and type 2 diabetes.

The ACPM recommends a diet similar to what the American Heart Association and the American Diabetes Association recommends: 55 percent of calories from carbohydrates, about 25 percent of calories from fat, and around 20 percent from protein. The Atkins diet differs, depending on which of four "phases" a dieter is in. The Atkins diet suggests (during the initial weight-loss phase, not the "maintenance" phase) 5 percent carbohydrates, 60 percent fat, and 35 percent protein. That's around the upper limit of protein recommendations that most other experts suggest.

Researchers argue that protein is not the real issue. The real problem with the Atkins diet is that it is unrestricted in trans and saturated fat, which are clearly the most harmful elements in the American diet. And it restricts foods that are health-promoting, such as whole grains.

Those who promote the Atkins plan say that restricting carbohydrates means the body must turn to fat and burn it for energy, resulting in weight loss, and that it has been proven to be better than other low-fat diets in terms of weight loss. It also cuts factors that can lead to heart disease. For instance, the diet raises levels of HDL cholesterol, the so-called "good" cholesterol. Atkins proponents also say that reducing carbohydrates and insulin production are the key to keeping insulin levels healthy and reducing diabetes risk.

However, the ACPM notes there's evidence that some high-fiber carbohydrate sources actually help maintain healthy insulin levels.

Regardless, fad diets of all types should be avoided. They do nothing but perpetuate a miserable cycle of losing and gaining until you just feel like a failure. As we discussed in the previous laws of leadership, keeping a positive attitude is imperative to your health.

I remember doing a segment on CNN about fad diets entitled, "Are They After Your Wallet or Your Waistline?" I ripped apart some popular diets on that segment. One of the diet programs I gave a thumbs-down to called me the next day. They were upset. I told them, "If you can get on your soapbox and tell a lie, I can get on my soapbox and tell the truth!" And I hung up the phone. I have seen so many fad diets prevent people who really want to achieve their goals from doing so.

The reason I went onto CNN every New Year's was to help people get on the right course and stay on course. Fad diets come out in droves at the first of the year and most of them are dead ends. I have seen so many people following a diet that doesn't work, and they put their whole heart into it.

A friend called me to ask if I could help a guy who was way overweight at over 500 pounds, but before I had a chance to meet with him, he tried a fad diet and died the second week he was on it. This is one of the reasons I intensely go after fad diets.

Let's keep it simple. Here is the question you have to ask yourself. Can you follow that fad diet for five years, 10 years achieving their goals achieving their goals–can you do it for 20 years? The answers to these questions should tell you if you should do it at all.

So my question to you is! Are you going to avoid fad diets, Yes or No?

Awesome! Let's move to The Nineteenth Health Law of Leadership.

"The fad diet question: can you follow it for 10 years, 20 years, and can you follow it for 30 years? The answer to this question tells you if you should follow it at all."

Jerry L. Anderson

The Nineteenth Health Law of Leadership

Set Realistic Weight Loss Goals!

I want you to set a realistic weight loss goal for yourself. Setting a goal to lose five pounds a week is setting yourself up for failure. People tell me they want to lose the weight quick. The problem with quick weight loss is, if you lose the weight fast and don't have healthy habits, you are going to gain the weight back. I am a firm believer that the longer it takes to lose the weight, the greater the habits you create.

I recommend you focus on losing a half a pound to a pound of fat a week. Think about it. If you lose half of pound of fat a week, that will be 26 pounds of weight loss in one year and five inches off your waistline. If you lose one pound of fat a week in one year, you will have a weight loss of at least 52 pounds, and that's about 10 inches off your waistline. You're not just after the weight loss. Your goal should be the long-term lifestyle change.

Determine your healthy waistline goal. For every inch you are over your goal, you need to lose five pounds. So if your waistline is to lose four inches, your weight loss goal should be about twenty pounds.

About one in three American adults is trying to lose weight at any given time, and while their track record for trying is good, their track record for succeeding is not.

Here is another reason you should set realistic goals:

Most dieters who don't will regain the weight they lost within five years.

Usually within five years, most dieters will regain the weight they lost. And, some studies have found that even more weight is gained after that five-year period of time. Insights into this phenomenon are beginning to show that unrealistic goals could be the culprit. Losing weight too fast is one of them. Most experts agree that a slow, steady loss of about one or two pounds a week is the best strategy.

Social pressures also contribute to failing diets. Boredom or feelings of deprivation can knock out your diet plan as well. Fast food menus don't help with healthier choices either, and some say healthy foods are less convenient or require more time and money to prepare. People also tend to underestimate the number of calories in foods and overestimate calories burned through exercise.

When trying to lose weight, rules become important to individuals in order to abide by your plan, i.e., self-laws. In one study, researchers asked 132 women trying to lose weight on their own to tell him their strategies—their dieting "rules," so to speak. In all, the 132 dieters offered 895 rules, with each woman listing an average of nearly seven. His research team followed the women to see which rules worked. Over all, adherence to the self-set rules was low. But the ones deemed most effective were the simplest—reducing calories and increasing exercise. Other rules that worked included: decreasing sugar intake, increasing consumption of fruits and vegetables, vitamins and water, watching less TV, and eating at home more often.

If you've tried unsuccessfully to diet many times, researchers recommend getting a coach. A coach can be your doctor, another health professional, or a friend who will hold you accountable to your goals. Recording your intake of calories every day, limiting calories, and exercising seven hours a week, including cardiovascular and weight workouts, will all help to achieve your goals and establish good habits.

One researcher compared people on the Weight Watchers, Atkins, Zone and Ornish diets and found no substantial weight-loss differences at one year, regardless of the diet. The amount of weight lost ranged from 4.6 to 7.3 pounds. Steering clear of fad diets and establishing rules and patterns for yourself are more effective strategies.

I talked to this one guy who told me that a 'biggest loser' contest was going on at his job. He had been drinking three liters of soda a day. When they started the contest, he stopped drinking the soda. He lost 50 pounds in 12 weeks and won the contest. After the contest, he gained all 50 pounds back in less than six weeks! His goal was only to win the contest, not to change his behavior. That's a lose-lose strategy.

The scale can also show signs of an emotional problem. One woman I coached was very heavy and only 21 years old. She said she was okay with her weight, though. When I put her on the scale, she weighed 300 pounds. When she saw that, she broke out crying. It wasn't pretty, and I was on damage control from that point on. When she got the real results of her behavior, it hit her hard. You can close your eyes to the scale, but when you open them, there might be tears coming down.

Believe me, I have been in emotional damage control situations quite often. Now I ask people, if I weigh you before we work out, will you be able to handle it emotionally? The short stick is, you can't drive your car without checking the gas gauge, you can't run your business without checking the books, and you don't know what's going on with your body unless you check the scale.

I met this guy who just joined the gym and on our first meeting, I checked his body weight, body fat, and muscle weight. It showed he was 60 pounds overweight. So I set up a plan to help him lose it. I gave him the choice to lose one or two pounds a week. He chose to lose two pounds a week and I told him it should take him about 30 weeks to achieve his goal.

The next day he came to me with a new plan. He said, "Coach Jerry, a friend of mine lost 60 pounds in 30 days and I'm going to follow what she did." I was blown away. I asked, "What is your weight loss plan?" He said his plan was to lose 60 pounds in 30 days. "How are you going to do this?" I asked, dumbfounded. He said he was going to eat 800 calories a day and do three hours of cardio a day. I couldn't believe it. He was 235 pounds. I wouldn't give my cat an 800-calories-a-day diet. He set himself up for failure! Do you know he only lasted five days on that program? I have not seen him at the gym since he set that crazy weight loss goal.

My question to you is, are you going to set realistic weight loss goals, Yes or No?

Awesome! Let's move to The Twentieth Health Law of Leadership.

"I'm a firm believer that, the longer it takes to lose the weight, the greater the habits you create."

The Twentieth Health Law of Leadership

Relax and Laugh!

I want you to spend at least 10 minutes every evening relaxing and laughing. Here's the reason. Relaxing and laughing will reduce your stress level and open up your blood vessels so they can deliver more blood, oxygen, and nutrients to your cells. This will recharge you back to 100 percent so you can be productive the next day. Here is an easy way to do it. Watch your favorite comedy show. Go to YouTube or pop in a video and relax and laugh.

Here is another reason you should relax and laugh:

Laughter is Ha-Ha-Heart-Healthy.

For the first time, researchers have found that laughter causes the endothelium, the inner lining of blood vessels, to dilate. This increases blood flow, which is good for overall cardiovascular health. A

135

cheap laugh really can improve your health! This advice pertains to watching comedies, not stress-provoking shows.

Although this is the first study to show that laughter has such an effect, the analysts noted that people with heart disease generally responded to everyday life events with less humor than people who were healthy. Harvard University researchers reported that people with an optimistic outlook also have a reduced risk of heart disease.

Twenty healthy volunteers were randomly assigned to watch 15 to 30 minutes of a light movie such as *Kingpin, Something About Mary* or excerpts from *Saturday Night Live*; or, on the heavier side, the Steven Spielberg war drama *Saving Private Ryan*. The participants were divided equally between men and women, averaged 33 years of age, and had had their initial blood flow measured after an overnight fast. A minimum of 48 hours later, the volunteers came back and watched a second movie they had not seen previously.

In this respect, the study eliminated confounding factors that could arise when comparing two separate individuals. During the sessions, researchers took 160 measurements of blood flow in the arm's brachial artery. Almost all of the volunteers (95 percent) experienced increased blood flow while watching the funny movie, while three quarters (74 percent) had decreased flow while observing the ravages of war onscreen. Over all, average blood flow increased 22 percent while laughing and decreased 35 percent during mental stress. The changes lasted 30 to 45 minutes after watching the movie segment.

The magnitude of the changes was similar to the benefits seen with aerobic activity, researchers said. That's *not* a reason to trade laughing for exercise though; the ideal would be to do both.

The endothelium has endorphin receptors (a feel-good chemical), so what is probably happening is that after a good laugh, these endorphins are released and activate the receptors. Mental stress may lead to the release of stress hormones such as cortisol, which may then reduce the release of nitric oxide (not to be confused with the laughing gas nitrous oxide) from endothelial cells. This, in turn, could constrict the vessels.

So, if anyone in your family complains you watch too much television, you can tell them you're doing it for your health!

The story I'm about to tell you is one of the worst cases of how your arteries can constrict and cut off the blood flow to your brain or heart. A friend of mine was telling me about someone she knew who had recently died. Her friend and her friend's husband were having an argument on Sunday morning while getting ready for church. In the middle of the argument, she got so mad she had a heart attack and died. The sad part of the story was her six children were standing right there watching them both argue before she passed out and died. When you are under high stress, it constricts your arteries and reduces the blood flow to your heart or brain. When your heart and brain become constricted, those areas can die.

I was sitting at my desk at the gym and this guy in workout clothes walks by. I called him over. "What do you do for a living?" I asked him. "I have seen a lot of people walk around this gym in the last 30 years, and you are the most stressed out person I've ever seen in my life!"

"How do you know I'm stressed?" he answered, defiantly.

"You look like you have a film of stress around your body," I said with concern. As it turns out, he was in charge of a sales team of 400 people. After I urged him to sit down and talk to me, he ended up signing up to start training. He turned out to be the greatest guy you'd ever want to meet once his stress level went down. A lot of his team members worked out in my gym, and frankly, they hated him. Apparently, he yelled and screamed during their meetings. "Kick his butt, Jerry! He's crazy," they said behind his back. This is another reason you need to relax and laugh every day. This man lost his personality from all the accumulated daily stressors.

One of the trainers at the gym checked the blood pressure of a customer. He didn't pass the test at 140/90. The health club had a policy that your blood pressure had to be under 120/80 to work out or you needed a doctor's release. The trainer then asked me to check it because the guy said his blood pressure is always normal. I went over and checked it and it was 140/90. "Relax for five minutes and we'll try again," I told him. I checked it again and it was still 140/90.

"What's your day been like?" I asked him, looking for clues.

"It was normal, but before I left, I had to fire two people," he admitted. I asked him if he thought that was the cause of his elevated blood pressure.

"No," he insisted. "I have been doing my job for 30 years and if people don't produce, I fire them."

"I hear what you're saying, but from a physical standpoint, it's showing something different," I told

139

him. In his mind, firing two people had no impact on him, but in his body, it showed in the constriction of his arteries and increased blood pressure. We parted ways, but not before I reminded him how important it is to relax and laugh after a stressful event or day.

One of my clients was telling me that her husband had come home from work one night and passed out at the front door. She thought he had died. He'd been working from 5 a.m. to 10 p.m. every night for the last six months. She called 911 and the paramedics revived him and took him to the hospital. He was there for 10 days until his vital signs stabilized. "He was overworked and stressed out," she said sadly, remembering the event.

When you are under high stress, your arteries contract and this reduces the blood flow to your brain. This blood flow feeds oxygen and nutrients to it. His arteries had constricted so much, they cut off the blood flow to his brain and he passed out and almost died.

My question to you is, are you going to Relax and Laugh, Yes or No?

Awesome! Let's move to The Twenty First Health Laws of Leadership, the last law of leadership.

"Relaxing and laughing will reduce your stress level, open up your blood vessels, and recharge you for the next day."

Jerry L. Anderson

The Twenty-First Health Law of Leadership

Visualize Yourself Succeeding!

I want you to visualize yourself succeeding. Take five minutes every morning and visualize yourself following the 21 Health Laws of Leadership. If you can visualize it, you can actualize it.

Here are a few more reasons you should visualize yourself succeeding following the 21 Health Laws of Leadership.

In a classic study completed in the 1920s at the University of Chicago, three groups of basketball-playing students were tested on how accurately they shot free throws. They were then given different instructions. One group was to practice, one group not to practice, and one group to just visualize themselves shooting baskets without picking up a ball and doing it. After 20 days, the group that had not practiced did not show any improvement, the group that practiced improved by 24 percent, and the group that used visualization improved by 23 percent.

Research has revealed that mental practices are almost as effective as true physical practice, and that doing both is more effective than either alone. For instance, in his study on everyday people, Guang Yue, an exercise psychologist from the Cleveland Clinic Foundation, compared people who went to the gym with people who carried out virtual workouts in their heads. He found a 30 percent muscle increase in the group who went to the gym. However, the group of participants who conducted mental exercises of the weight training increased muscle strength by almost half as much (13.5 percent). This average remained for three months following the mental training.

Most interesting is that many experimental and clinical psychologists have proven beyond a shadow of a doubt that the human nervous system cannot tell the difference between an "actual" experience and an experience imagined vividly and in detail.

I was training this one woman for a competition and she was scared to death. It was her first contest and she had eight weeks left to train. I prompted her to start visualizing herself every day winning the contest, and by the day of the event, she will have visually experienced over fifty competitions with the power of visualization. The day of the competition came and when she got on stage, she wiped out the competition. Mental rehearsals can mean almost the same as doing what you are visualizing. The visualizing succeeded in making up for years of competition experience without ever competing because on that day, she commanded the stage like she'd spent her life there.

The first time I used the power of visualization in my life happened when I was in my mid-twenties. I wanted to win a bodybuilding contest, so I looked through some bodybuilding magazines and found a body I thought I could achieve. I cut it out of the magazine, took a photo of myself, cut my head out, and pasted it on the body I wanted to become from the magazine. Then I taped it on my bathroom mirror so I could see it every day.

When my friends and family members saw it, they laughed at it. Even the girl I was dating at the time took her shots at me. "That looks ridiculous," she said. "It's never going to happen." That didn't stop me. I kept visualizing that body every night and every morning. It took me five years to get that body, but I went on to win ten bodybuilding competitions in a row and the Mr. Natural Universe title.

Here's what *not* to do. I was speaking at a conference and sharing this story when a woman in the audience started crying. I was thinking, what did I say to upset her? After my presentation, I walked up to her and asked if I'd offended her in some way.

"No, not at all," she said. "The reason I started crying is because I realized something. I did the same thing you did but the exact opposite. I took a picture of myself overweight and put it on my refrigerator door. I thought it would stop me from overeating, but I ended up gaining more weight." If you create the wrong vision, you are going to produce the wrong results.

So my question to you is! Are you going to visualize yourself following The 21 Health Laws of Leadership, Yes or No?

Awesome! This is the last Health Law of Leadership.

"Visualize yourself following the 21 Health Laws of Leadership every morning, then walk into that vision every day."

CONCLUSION

Your Health is the Foundation of Leadership

Congratulations! You have just read through *The Leadership Diet, The 21 Health Laws of Leadership*. Now you're ready to start implementing these laws into your life. Learn them, apply them and they will improve your health.

I have been teaching health for over 30 years and during that time, I have asked all the people I coached, trained, and spoken to this one question I am going to ask you now: Can you lead your business, your congregation, or your family without your health? This is why I am a firm believer that: Your health is the foundation of leadership.

Let's not forget about the current health condition of most leaders. Studies have shown that 82 percent of leaders were found to be considered overweight, 36 percent of leaders were found to have high blood pressure, 13 percent of leaders were found to be diabetic, 23 percent of leaders were found to have high cholesterol, 70 percent of leaders were found to be in poor physical condition, 60 percent were unable to touch their toes, 62 percent were unable to do a single push up or sit up, and 28 percent had never exercised since their childhood.

The good news is that the majority of these health issues may be reduced or eliminated by following the 21 Health Laws of Leadership. Use the laws that are going to have the greatest impact on your health. You probably don't need to follow all of them, but they will serve you well if you do.

I pray that you do it for yourself. I pray that you do it for your team. I pray that you do it for your congregation. I pray that you do it for your family. And I pray that you do it so you can become the healthy leader God created you to be.

SOURCES

Ades, P.A. and Coello, C.E. *Effects of Exercise and Cardiac Rehabilitation on Cardiovascular Outcomes.* Medical Clinics of North America 84(1):251-264

American College of Cardiology scientific sessions, Orlando, Florida

David Celermajer, Ph.D., M.B.B.S., researcher, University of Sydney, Australia; Aug. 15, 2006, Journal of the American College of Cardiology; Jeanne Moloo, R.D., Ph.D., Sacramento, California, dietitian and spokeswoman, American Dietetic Association

David Celermajer, Ph.D., M.B.B.S., researcher, University of Sydney, Australia; Aug. 15, 2006, Journal of the American College of Cardiology; Jeanne Moloo, R.D., Ph.D., Sacramento, Calif., dietitian and spokeswoman, American Dietetic Association

Jerry L. Anderson

Columbia University, Mailman School of Public Health, news release, April 29, 2011

Cornell University, news release, June 17, 2015

Michael Dansinger, M.D., assistant professor, medicine, Tufts-New England Medical Center, Boston; Barbel Knauper, Dr.Phil., associate professor, psychology, McGill University, Montreal, Canada; *Journal of the American Medical Association*, Jan. 5, 2005

European Society of Endocrinology, news release, May 7, 2012

Exercise and fatigue: Physical Activity. National Library of Medicine Medical Encyclopedia.

Exercise: A Healthy Habit to Start and Keep. American Academy of Family Physicians.

Exercise and Fitness Health Library Copyright ©2016 LimeHealth. All Rights Reserved.

Bamini Gopinath, Ph.D., associate professor, Centre for Vision Research, department of ophthalmology, Westmead Institute for Medical Research, University of Sydney, Australia; Lona Sandon, Ph.D., R.D., program director and assistant professor, clinical nutrition, school of health professions, University of Texas Southwestern Medical Center at Dallas; *Journals of Gerontology,* online, June 1, 2016

150

William A. Gray, M.D., assistant professor, clinical medicine, Columbia University College of Physicians and Surgeons, director, endovascular services, Center for Interventional Vascular Therapy at New York-Presbyterian Hospital/Columbia University Medical Center, New York City, and co-director, Transcatheter Cardiovascular Therapeutics; Robert Restaino, doctoral student, department of medical pharmacology and physiology, University of Missouri, Columbia, Missouri; July 2015, Experimental Physiology

Harvard Men's Health Watch, news release, February 2005

Imperial College London, news release, Feb. 22, 2017

Just Move. American Heart Association.

David Katz, M.D., co-author, American College of Preventive Medicine (ACPM) policy statement, member of the ACPM Board of Regents, and director, Prevention Research Center, Yale University School of Medicine, New Haven, Conn.; Colette Heimowitz, director, education and research, Atkins Health & Medical Information Services, New York City; Feb. 19-23, 2003, ACPM annual meeting, San Diego

Vasanti Malik, ScD, nutrition research scientist, Harvard T.H. Chan School of Public Health, Boston; Marina Chaparro, RDN, CDE, MPH, clinical dietitian and certified diabetes educator, Joe DiMaggio Children's Hospital, Hollywood, Florida.; William Dermody Jr., vice president, policy, American Beverage Association; *Journal of the American College of Cardiology*, Sept. 28, 2015

Mayo Clinic Proceedings, news release, March 12, 2014

Michael Miller, M.D., director, preventive cardiology, University of Maryland Medical Center, and associate professor, medicine, University of Maryland School of Medicine, Baltimore; Richard Hayes, M.D., clinical assistant professor, medicine, New York University Medical Center, New York City; March 7, 2005, Presentation.

Weight Lifting to Lose Weight By Ingfei Chen American College of Sports Medicine.

Image Source:
http://www.heandshefitness.com/2017/01/19/the-5-key-steps-to-eliminating-visceral-body-fat/

Want to Book

Health Coach Jerry

At Your

Next Event?

Please email: Jerry2motivate@yahoo.com with the following information:

Your company name

Your name and contact information

The dates you are requesting

Your budget

We will promptly reply to your request!

Health Coach Jerry will discuss how he can meet the best of what you need and want for your people.

Jerry is also available to speak on radio or as a guest on television. Call Jerry at 562.794.7174

Website: www.healthspeakerjerryanderson.com

FREE

COACHING

SESSION

SPECIAL OFFER

FREE SESSION with every eleven sessions purchased.

Push yourself to reach your health goals with Leadership Health Coach Jerry Anderson. You will work one-on-one with Jerry to develop a success plan that clearly states your goals and defines the steps you need to get there. Using the 21 Health Laws of Leadership developed by Jerry Anderson over the last thirty years, you will discover strategies for overcoming the obstacles in your way. Team up with Health Coach Jerry and start achieving your Health goals today!

CALL NOW AND SCHEDULE YOUR APPOINTMENT!

With Health Coach Jerry (562) 794-7174

Email: Jerry2motivate@yahoo.com